SCHOOL'S OUT!
IT'S SUMMER!

School's Out!

It's Summer!

Joan M. Bergstrom

Ten Speed Press
Berkeley, California

1🖉 Ten Speed Press
Box 7123
Berkeley, Ca 94707

Text and cover design by Fifth Street Design, Berkeley CA

Cover photography: Comstock Inc. and Comstock Inc., David Lokey

Illustrations: Tina Cash, Mark Ziemann, and Richard Walsh

Library of Congress Cataloging-in-Publication Data
Bergstrom, Joan.
    School's Out! It's Summer! / Joan Bergstrom.
       p. cm.
    Includes bibliographical references.
    ISBN 0-89815-463-4
    1. Child rearing—United States. 2. Creative activities and seat work. 3. Family recreation—United States. I. Title.
    HQ769.B5183 1992   91-38910
    649'.68'0973—dc20   CIP

First Printing, 1992

Printed in the United States of America

1 2 3 4 5—96 95 94 93 92

CONTENTS

Acknowledgments

Thanks and More Thanks.

Over the years my work on children's use of out-of-school time has been supported by many generous, far-sighted, and creative people. Children, parents, grandparents, sitters, educators, recreation staff, and others have been gracious in sharing their insights, expertise, and experiences with me.

There are many that I have turned to for help in preparing this book. Eric Hayot played a very central and important editorial role. Eric was always ready with innovative insights and creative ways to consider or reconsider the presentation of an idea. He often assisted me in the clarification of a topic at hand. His talented editing was a major contribution to the creation of this book. Thanks and many thanks to the team at Ten Speed: Mariah Bear and Sal Glynn spent hours helping to shape the manuscript. They both made suggestions that helped to make many points clearer and easier for the reader. George Young continues to be one of the most patient people I know. His keen questions always help me distill and articulate what I know. At times I wonder how he can avoid becoming exasperated with me. Phil Wood, as always, is one of the most casual and poignant teachers that I have. Brent Beck at Fifth Street Design worked hard to make the manuscript into a friendly and inviting book for families to use. He searched tirelessly for appropriate illustrations and I always had the sense that he would come up with the right solution to any problem. Thanks to a tremendous team.

I hope that you have a fun and fanciful summer with your family. Remember to trust your intuition and be kind to yourself.

You Can Have A Celebrated Summer

Closing assembly is over, and happy children stream out the dirty-gray doors of the school gym. At their lockers, kids pack their bookbags for the last time. Everyone is talking; voices fill the air and sometimes a phrase, shouted louder than the rest, cuts through the din: "Have a great summer." "See you in September." "Where are you going?" "For how long?"

Summer. For most kids, it means three months of freedom after nine long months of school. Many see it as a time to do absolutely nothing, but summer can be even more fun when there are lots of things for kids to do. Going to camp, visiting relatives, swimming with friends, and other typical summer activities can help your child to learn, grow, explore, and become good at something this summer.

Are you dreading the first time (about four days into summer vacation) that your child walks into the living room or calls you at work and sighs, "There's nothing to do"? What can you do to make this a fun, fantastic, fabulous summer for your child—without killing yourself in the process?

Why Is Summer So Important?

If you add up all of the hours a child spends out of school during afternoons, weekends, and vacations in an average year, you'll discover that they comprise almost 80 percent of that child's waking time. This unstructured time, equal to 4,680 out-of-school hours a year or 195 twenty-four-hour days, occurs during one of the most important developmental stages of your child's life. Summer accounts for almost half of that time.

MAKE THIS SUMMER A MEMORABLE ONE

Since the last month of school is often a preparation for summer and the first month is generally review, summer actually extends over five months. Some school systems across the country *are* working on a year-round calendar that gives students less time off in the summer, but even these children can benefit from a change of routine, time to play, and exposure to different kinds of activities.

Over summer break, even the most active and motivated child will spend some time in front of the TV, talking on the phone, or just "hanging out." What makes children who *celebrate* their summers special is that they spend much of their time actively doing something—these kids understand that summer time is a precious and valuable resource which shouldn't be wasted.

It is never too soon for you to start thinking about your child's summer, and if you're thinking about it, your child should be thinking about it too. Involving children in their summer plans takes only a little more time than making choices for them, and often keeps both parties much happier. Strive for a collaborative rather than a one-sided planning process.

The single greatest challenge may be seeing summer as an opportunity instead of a source of constant difficulty. Summer offers a huge block of unstructured time, and that can be threatening as well as exciting. Parents often resist planning because they want summer to be relaxed and unhurried. They imagine a spontaneous, fun-filled time— but this romantic ideal is often shattered ten days into summer: The TV is on all the time, wet swimsuits are strewn about the house, kids are fighting over who gets the last popsicle, and everyone is looking for something to do. Your child's summer needs to be broken up by more than the daily arrival of the ice cream truck—children need and usually appreciate routines and structure.

Eileen, now a graduate student, found an activity one summer that changed her life. "Every morning when I was ten," she said, "I would recite, 'Mom, I'm bored—what can I do today?' My mother's usual response was, 'You can read and do things in the house while I'm gone.' One day Mom saw an ad in the local newspaper announcing free tennis lessons. She enrolled me, and I spent every day that summer playing tennis.

"Those free tennis lessons were the basis for developing concentration, good sportsmanship, discipline, physical endurance, and lifelong friendships. Every time I walk into the house and see the piano covered with trophies, I'm reminded of how my mother, who has since died, did me a great favor by finding that ad in the newspaper."

Your kids can use this dense, uninterrupted block of time to make a great deal of progress on one or two activities or interests they really love. Children often get excited when they can see themselves progress rapidly, and funnel that excitement back into their interests. Children gain self-confidence when they can take pride in how well they make things, or perform, or in how much they know.

All parents want their children to have memorable summers. You can help your child have a summer worth celebrating by giving her free time to relax while still guiding her toward activities she'll enjoy. These activities can develop independence while teaching her to use free time with responsibility, resourcefulness, and creativity. So start thinking early, let summer plans simmer, mix in equal parts of free time and organized activities, and you'll be well on your way to a celebrated summer.

The Ingredients of a Summer of Celebration

✔ *Allow your child to be part of the planning process.* Children should help decide what they will do and when and how they will do it for either some days of the week or some weeks of the summer. School-age children do best at activities when they have shared in planning them.

✔ *Give your child the chance to prepare, anticipate, recollect, and celebrate a special project or two.* Your child needs to be able to plan ahead with you what the family is going to do and then look forward to it with great anticipation. Later, the family should be able to look back through certificates, programs, photos, and letters and enjoy the summer all over again. Celebrating the summer when it's gone helps your child think about the things he did or learned and how he changed during those months.

✔ *Your child needs to do different things during the summer.* For many families, successful summers are divided into four parts: time at home, time using community resources, time at camp, and an excursion or vacation. Balancing these four will give your child a more creative and interesting summer.

✔ *The best summer routines are those that liberate, not constrain.* Flexibility is an essential element of every good summer. Combining flexible and structured activities gives your child time to play, learn, experiment, explore, and be with others. A child's vacation should not be explicitly laid out minute by minute; he needs open spans of time to do his own thing and relax.

✔ *Provide opportunities to try and to do new and exciting things.* Trips, adventures, meeting new people, learning about new subjects, collecting mementos and knicknacks, trying new foods, sleeping in new beds, hearing new noises, and gaining new skills all add to the enjoyment and celebration of summer.

✔ *Summer is also the perfect time to expand on current interests.* Children can use this time to renew old friendships, get better at games, or practice an instrument.

✔ *Going to camp is a great way for your child to learn and grow outside the home.* Specialty camps, like space camps, environmental and nature camps, or football camps can foster one particular interest, while general camps let your kid discover new and different things such as arts and crafts, sports, or camping and hiking.

✔ *Continue to help your child develop the other 3 Rs: resourcefulness, responsibility, and reliability.* These are critical aspects of growing up. Parents can help children develop independence by establishing routines, encouraging chores, guiding viewing of television and video, playing games or reading on rainy days, and teaching summer safety.

✔ *Make sure your child's summer activities reflect your values.* Generally, parents are most interested in summer activities and experiences that encourage fun, foster creativity, promote independence, and teach something other than what is learned in school. Make sure your aims for your child's summer are clear.

✔ *Decide what your child means when she complains of having "nothing to do."* Children often do this out of habit; they may be asking for your help organizing their time or just hoping that you'll go running to the video store to rent a movie. Talk with your child about ways to spend time when there is no structured activity going on.

✔ *Recognize your limits as a parent.* Most parents are extremely busy, even during the summer, and may not have time to drive their kids to practice every day at 7 a.m. Don't schedule so many activities or adventures that no one in the family has any time alone; trying to do too much can leave you and your child miserable.

✔ *Develop an "authoritative" parenting style.* "Authoritative" parents are neither too lenient nor too strict; they establish clear limits, articulate their wishes, and don't give in to unreasonable demands. Conflict is handled by a negotiation process in which parents and children exchange ideas to reach a mutually agreeable solution. When your child is a part of the decision-making process, everyone involved will be more comfortable discussing and researching summer resources and more confident that the activity you do choose in the end is the right one.

These goals might look like too much to handle, but if you plan ahead and work with your child, everything should fall into place. Don't worry if your child doesn't find a keen interest this summer. It is more important that he discover a slate of experiences and friendships that will send him back to school more confident and more interesting. When kids or adults talk about summer, the ones who did something interesting *are* more interesting; a conversation that begins "What did you do?" "Oh, nothing," ends as quickly as it starts. Children who do "nothing" often become adults who do "nothing."

Remember that your child can have an interesting summer without climbing Everest or enrolling in flight school—all you need to do is guide, plan, and encourage and your child's summer will be terrific.

Summer and the Years of Opportunity

Children between the ages of six and twelve have tremendously different energy levels, attention spans, personalities, and interests. Some themes, however, stay constant for most kids in this period, known as "middle childhood." An awareness of these general tendencies will help you make better summer plans.

Children are <u>intensely social</u> during these years, seeking other children to make and develop friendships. Children this age love game-playing; some experts even call this the "gang period," because children develop such strong ties among their peers. They often want to visit each other's houses, see each other's rooms and outdoor spaces, spend the night, and go places together.

Being with other children lets your child sort out what the world is like and how he fits into it. This may include learning to change his behavior to get along with other kids; realizing when he is being too wild, too pompous, too silly, or too shy. Children in groups gradually gauge and adjust their ways of talking and acting to make and keep friends.

Between the ages of eight-and-a-half and ten, a child often finds a "best friend" for the first time. With this best friend or buddy (usually of the same sex), the child develops a real sensitivity to what matters to others. As such friendships develop, children start to think about ways to make their friend happy.

Summer also gives children time to make new friends under the relaxed conditions of one long recess. Since summer friendships usually involve cooperating or collaborating on activities, these friendships encourage children to invest time in new projects or try new sports. Some summer friendships are rekindled every year when school lets out.

Cognitive growth progresses quickly in this period, fueled by the child's burning curiosity and excitement about learning. Reading opens new worlds to children, and they absorb astonishing amounts of factual information. They talk constantly, describing scenes and people, telling interminable stories, recounting detailed information, and playing with their expanding vocabularies. Children between six and nine are fascinated by classifications and often memorize vast systems of information—kinds of dinosaurs, names of Greek gods, species of birds—while constantly sorting smaller bits of knowledge into categories. Daniel, an eight-year-old, looking out a window with binoculars, came up with a steady stream of observations, thoughts, and questions:

"There's a katydid down there. Did you know that hummingbirds can't walk? Hey! (using binoculars) I've got a nice, big, plump robin. (Puts binoculars down.) I wonder if it's raining in China. We could call the weather in China. I wish the scarlet tanagers would come back. They're so neat. Mom, where's Arizona? Where's Wyoming?—wild and wooly and wacky Wyoming."

Their rapidly developing motor skills give children a growing sense of independence and self-esteem. School-age children enjoy displays of prowess, and play vigorously at four-square, tennis, basketball, gymnastics, and other sports.

Children in this age group tend to bounce back quickly from setbacks. They may get sad, or angry, or upset, but they usually get over these feelings quickly. Children this age are a lot of fun for adults to be with, but while they seem "easy" compared to preschoolers or adolescents, they still need guidance and support.

Many times, however, your children can guide and support themselves. Play is a natural and spontaneous experience, especially for children between six and twelve. A city block swarming with children on a hot summer afternoon overflows with examples of children's ingenuity and creativity. Two children sit on a stoop playing a card game while two others weave potholders. On the sidewalk, four girls are jumping rope and chanting songs, and on the corner others are squirting each other with a hose. All of these children are having pure fun, seizing the moment, learning how to be friends, collaborating, cooperating, exercising, understanding what makes a good sport, and experiencing their neighborhood.

All children need plenty of chances for just "going outside to play." Time for daydreaming, dressing up, getting into mischief, talking to oneself, playing in a brook, and generally messing around is at the very heart of childhood. Children also enjoy playing games like Monopoly or Hail to the Chief, which challenge them to understand and remember complicated rules. But even when children tell jokes, throw water balloons, or just act silly, they can be making good use of their time.

The summer is a great time for your child to pursue special interests with an influential adult such as a sitter, friend, grandparent, or other relative. Having an older friend to work with often keeps a child interested and excited.

Ben, who was the editor of his college paper, taught his younger brother Timmy writing and editing skills one summer. Timmy was ten years younger than Ben and keenly interested in journalism. Every week Ben assigned Timmy a project. During an eight-week period Timmy wrote several short stories and assisted Ben on journalism assignments.

Going off to camp is the highlight of some kids' summers, while for others it is a dreadful experience. Children in the second group rarely talk about anything except how horrible the camp was. For those who enjoy camp, however, it can be a foundation for a lifetime of activities.

MIX A FEW
INGREDIENTS
FOR A SUMMER
OF CELEBRATIONS

Dale started going to summer camp when he was seven years old. He lived in a big city during the year and loved to play outdoors during the summer. At camp, he tried all the activities: swimming, boating, waterskiing, tennis, softball, baseball, soccer, archery, arts and crafts, and drama. He made strong friendships with his bunkmates over the summer and insisted on going back every year.

At fifteen, when he could no longer be a camper, Dale became a counselor-in-training. After that, he was a counselor for three years; then, he trained the younger counselors. When he was twenty-one, Dale became an assistant head counselor; he organized and was captain of the camp "Olympics." Now a lawyer, Dale says the friends he made at summer camp are friends for life. Sharing a bunk with others taught him to compromise and share, to help others, and to be a team player.

Dale feels that his camp experience even helped prepare him for college; unlike many freshmen, he had already glimpsed living away from home and sharing his space with others. Dale still keeps in touch with his friends from summer camp.

Kids certainly don't have to leave home to have a good time. Parents' workplaces and communities often sponsor day camps. Riding to camp or work with a parent makes a child feel important and helps develop her relationship with that parent. Listening to your kid tell stories about how great her day was as you drive home is a natural way for you to stay in touch with her summer.

☆ ☆ ☆

Leslie had a great time going to the camp at her father's work. Children went swimming and took day trips to museums, parks, shopping centers, and the like. "It was so much fun," Leslie said. "I like that place. And for our last day, we went rollerskating and bowling."

☆ ☆ ☆

Robert, age twelve, dreaded the idea of going off to camp for one more summer. "I really hate that camp," he told his parents. "Everything is awful about it—the beds, the counselors, the kids, the bugs." He was determined not to go, but his parents were anxious for him to have a productive summer. Nearly every night that winter the family's dinner conversation focused on the heated topic of Robert and the wonderful camp. Finally, one night in early May his parents said, "If you can tell us what you would really like to do and how you propose to do it, we'll consider it."

Robert loved photography and swimming and arranged to take underwater photography lessons twice a week. On a third day, he would attend a photograph lecture series. Impressed, his parents agreed to give it a try. That summer, Robert read books featuring photographs of people, cities, and animals; *National Geographic* became his favorite magazine. He also went to the lake to swim when there were guards on duty. Everyone Robert worked with became excited about his interests, his desire to follow through, and his level of enthusiasm.

That summer gave Robert the time to be an active learner, explorer, discoverer, experimenter, and doer while deeply involved in two specific activities *he* had chosen. His parents helped by letting him have a say in his own plans and then helping him organize a summer around what he wanted to do.

Having a best friend of the same age is part of a fun and productive summer for many children, since two children often encourage each other to pursue mutual interests as they learn and grow together.

Heather, age eleven, reported that she and her friend Amy had a fabulous summer. Three times a week, Amy and Heather and a sitter worked together designing birthday cards, making book marks, and creating colorful small bags and wrapping papers. They also went to shops and other places to look for design ideas for their cards and bags. To make it more fun, the sitter would sometimes suggest a theme for the trip. For example, one week they focused on sailboats and the ways they were shown on cards, paper, boxes, T-shirts, and lots of other things. They would then go back and all work together. "It was great," Heather said. "I think I'm as good an artist as a lot of those that you see around the waterfront downtown. Wait, I want to show you the new hat I just designed for my cat José."

Vacations and excursions of various kinds are often a child's favorite summer memories. Whether you go somewhere on a plane, pack up and go camping, visit an amusement park, go fishing, or take the bus to a nearby lake, even one day away from the ordinary can be an exciting experience.

Claire, age ten, and her brother Nathan, age eight, love going on a trip each summer with their dad. Last year they spent three weeks in Colorado, swimming, horseback-riding, bike-riding, mountain-climbing, and more.

"We go on awesome trips with Dad," Claire said. "Every time he calls I ask him, 'Have you decided where we're going next?' "

Some kids discover that a community program becomes the highlight of their summer. Joey said he goes to the beach with his cousins and likes to go fishing with his dad during the summer. But "basketball camp was the best thing I did," he said. Camp was on Tuesday and Thursday nights, proving that you don't have to invest a huge amount of time to make an important memory. Joey's parents were able to help him have a great summer by simply using programs already going on in their community.

Many children, like Joey, prefer to concentrate on sports instead of quiet activities. "I really hate to read, you know," said Kylee. "But I like to ride my bike and go real far." Kylee's mother wanted her to attend a summer library program, however, so Kylee went and read or watched videos. Early in the fall she said, "I liked the program but I still don't like to read. You know that—I already told you. But the videos were really great."

Like Kylee's library program, not every activity you plan will be a stunning success. But offering your child the chance to diversify and explore new activities helps her define her interests. What does your child want to do again? What wouldn't your child like to do again next summer?

Your Child's Precious Summer Time

Summer never slides smoothly into fall; it comes to a screeching halt, perhaps because fun-filled summers go by so quickly, and are so different from school. Summer time is a precious commodity—it is the currency a child has to spend, and it should not be wasted.

Sociologist Elliott Medrich develops this analogy between time and money by comparing the use of children's time to "patterns of consumption." He argues that parents' decisions about how children spend their time reflect the particular family's values, priorities, and aspirations. Furthermore, Medrich points out that children's time, like money for most of us, is a finite resource. Children have only a certain amount of time available to spend.

Most parents teach their children not to waste money, but to spend it wisely on things that matter. Similarly, you can give your child guidance in how to spend his summer inventively, enjoyably, and wisely.

Children differ greatly in their health, education, housing, money, social experience, and access to camp programs or community resources. The one resource they have in common is time—the great equalizer. Across all social classes, children have the same number of hours to be eight years old. What your child does with her time is what makes her different from other kids. Parents who help their children have a fun, interesting, and somewhat productive summer give them a great advantage.

Don't underestimate your ability to monitor your child's time and help him decide how to spend it. Understanding how quickly time passes gives you a greater perspective on childhood than your kids, and you *can* decide to make their childhood count. As one mother put it, "I didn't want my daughter to look back and say, 'I didn't do much this summer. I'm glad it's over.' I didn't want summer to slip away, and to think later, 'Oops, we missed our chance.'"

Many parents have a limited amount of time to spend with their children, and some of the suggestions in this book may be a bit daunting for those parents. But the suggestions that follow are just that—*suggestions*. This book doesn't suggest that you immediately complete every list and every chart, buy every book, do every activity, go to every camp, watch every recital, secretly videotape your child while he plays, and learn every lesson, because if you do, everyone in your family will end up miserable and exhausted and as confused as this sentence. And that's exactly what you don't want.

A GIANT CALENDAR HELPS EVERYONE KEEP TRACK OF SUMMER PLANS

Pulling It All Together

Summer starts out as a huge block of totally unstructured time, and your child needs your help to plan it out. Planning the summer well ahead of time gives children a sense of control. They will be able to understand where the time goes, and look back on it later with some sense of excitement and accomplishment.

Filling out a giant calendar with your kid is a great way to make keeping track of time both visual and accessible. Planning out weekly routines and big trips or dates for camp ahead of time helps your child understand the rhythms of each week and the ebb and flow of summer time. It also gives the child a sense of anticipation about upcoming activities. Remember that you don't have to fill every block of time, that children need some unstructured time to wind down.

Start with a piece of heavy paper and draw a grid for each month. Children and parents can begin to fill in their schedules week by week. You can either set up a separate calendar for each child in the family, or make a whole family calendar where everyone—including parents—writes down their summer schedule. Calendars help children value rather than dread their free time because they learn to see time in perspective, as part of an overall summer pattern.

If you let your child design and make the calendar on his own, he may learn more from the experience. As he copies down dates from another calendar and writes in scheduled classes and meaningful reminders on his own, he will be learning about how time is organized, figuring out what will be going on during week one, week two, week three, and so on. (Be aware that the week after school lets out and the week before it starts up again are times when your kid will need a break or something fun to do. Unfortunately, these times are often some of the hardest for parents since school programs have just ended and summer ones haven't started yet.)

Referring to the calendar each day will give children a sense of control over their own activities, responsibilities, and even moods. You can review the next day's activities with each child in the evening and remind them what the day will hold each morning. You can also try making a week-at-a-glance plan. Looking at the calendar gives your child the security of seeing her routine written down and knowing she can always check it and see how it shapes a given week. Calendars like these can also help sitters plan fun activities with your child.

Many families like to put a monthly calendar in the middle of a bulletin board and surround it with useful information or artwork. Some of the information can be fairly permanent and fixed, such as emergency phone numbers. Other things you might post include: a list of books for summer reading, things to do when bored, recipes for nutritious no-bake snacks, and the family summer safety rules. Be sure to update these reminders as necessary.

You can use the calendar to write down things that your child liked about certain days, or give him appropriate stickers to put on especially bad or especially fun days. When the summer is over, your child can look back at the fun times he's had and put the calendar in a box of summer memories.

Another way to celebrate this summer is by helping your child take great photos, create a fun scrapbook, or design and make a box to store mementos like postcards, shells, stickers, stamps, baseball caps, or zany little plastic animals.

Creating a scrap book and/or decorated box for summer memories is a favorite project for many kids. Your child can keep track of his baseball games, make a list of favorite foods, or save tickets from an amusement park, airplane, train, or bus, collect menus, placemats, or coasters from favorite restaurants, and take or draw pictures of the best and worst things that happened. A "memory box" could also include one or two books that your child read and enjoyed over the summer and his own drawings about the book.

JULY

Sunday	Monday	Tuesday	Wednesday	Thursday	Friday	Saturday
			1	2	3	4
5	6 Jason and take train	7 Jen go to Grandma and from South Station	8	9 Uncle Bob's 9 am Monday	10	11 Jason and Jen back 4:00 pm
12	13 Gail to sit	14 Jason bikeriding with Paul Jen at home	15 Gail to sit	16 swimming at lake with Gail	17 around town with Gail	18
19 Picnic with Carey's at lake	20 Gail to sit	21 Gail to sit Jason and Jen baseball 5pm	22 ?	23 Swimming at lake with Gail	24 Family vacation starts! ☺	25 Family vacation ☺
26 Family	27 Family vacation	28 Gail to sit Jason and	29 Go to claypit for clay	30 Swimming at lake with Gail	31	

Since many six- to twelve-year-olds don't like to write, here are some other ways for children to keep track of their summers:

- ✔ Have your child create a record of her summer using photos, drawings, sculptures, and audio or video recordings of special events and memories. At the end of the summer, your child can set up an exhibit to describe her summer experience to relatives and friends and help the whole family remember it. This exhibit can stay in her bedroom or a family room for weeks, making the transition back to school easier.

- ✔ Collect photos of favorite events, places, friends, and any special experiences in a photo album. Even a month or so later you can look back at and talk about pictures of that Fourth of July when everyone got dressed up, or the time the family went off to pick raspberries and the container fell over and half the raspberries went back in the bushes. Kids can also take pictures of their own drawings and sculptures just in case something gets torn or broken. At the end of summer, you might add the charts from this book that you filled out together.

- ✔ Many kids find it exciting to keep a tape-recorded diary. Your child might prefer to record stories about only the fun things—the great picnic—or at least the interesting ones—like the time someone got lost on the boat trip.

- ✔ Your child could create a giant commemorative poster called "Summer of ____," using photos and drawings.

Next year, pull out all of this memorabilia and begin your planning session by asking your child, "What does this tell us about you? And what does it tell us about what you can do *this* summer?"

This book will help ensure that, come September, your child not only regrets that summer is over but is looking forward to the next one. In addition, you should be able to look back and say, "That was a great summer. It was fun, it was exciting, and it was enjoyable. It was the best summer we've had."

Helping Your Child Decide What To Do

Tuning In To Your Child's Interests

Figuring out exactly what your child wants to do may, at times, feel like following a trail of bread crumbs through a forest. Particularly with younger kids, who say they want to do everything, it's easy to follow a false trail and end up lost. If, however, you listen carefully to what your child says, watch her at play, and think about what you most enjoyed about your own childhood, you will find that coming up with a plan for your child's summer is rewarding for all concerned.

It is very important to discuss the options with your kid; to make him the central focus of your planning. Your input is very important; your child's doubly so.

In families with several children, there will have to be some give and take. Each child may not be able to pursue his or her burning interest to the extent desired. Transportation, time, money, and human and community resources must be considered.

The following six steps can help you tune in to your child's interests and begin planning a fun summer. These exercises will help you choose which community resources, camps, or other programs to investigate, and get you started planning a few excursions or a summer vacation. Once you know what your child is interested in, you know what sports equipment, art supplies, or games and backyard activities will be most fun for your family. *Don't* try to plan a whole summer in one night, though. Just think about a few issues at a time.

Step 1: Intuitions—Trust Them

Much of what you do as a parent is intuitive, based on love of your children and a desire for them to have a rich, enjoyable, and productive childhood. Thanks to years of experience, you know best how to interpret your child's behavior, signs of happiness, excitement, eagerness, frustration, fatigue, overstimulation, loneliness, and boredom.

JANE'S FAVORITE THINGS TO DO
* Play tapes
* Play cards
* Do 1001-piece puzzles
* Make paper airplanes
* Play with dolls

No one knows your child better than you. You know your child's strengths, temperament, and needs. Your instincts about what will interest your child are sound; use them. Trust your intuitions.

All parents, even those who are gone much of the time, are actively involved in their children's interests. In the middle of fixing breakfast, a parent may think about an exciting and simple summer outing; after dinner a father can get a team together to finish painting a fence; your discussion of a relative who's just been to Mexico can ignite an interest in soccer or fishing.

In the most ordinary, routine ways, you influence what your child believes. Even the most subtle, unplanned behavior establishes the chemistry of a household. You might not always recognize the ways you teach a young child about being a grown-up, but you should be aware that you are his major source of information and feedback on both his interests *and* your interests.

"A Portrait of My Child" is a series of questions that will help you get a handle on your intuitive knowledge of your child's temperament, needs, strengths, and aspirations. Remember, you know your child best.

A Portrait of My Child

1. How would you describe your child's temperament? What are your child's strengths? Weaknesses? What are your child's likes? Dislikes?

2. Do you have a sense that your child is an interesting person? Why?

3. Have your child's interests changed over time? How? Why?

4. Did your child seem to have enough to do last summer? What did you learn from last summer?

5. What are the high points of summer for your child? What are the low points? Why?

6. Did anything happen last summer that was painful or negative for your child? Did she learn anything from it? What did you learn from it?

7. In what area does your child seem to need the most help? Is there anything you can do about it this summer?

8. Has your child become involved with something because of a friend? Is it turning out to be a good experience for your child? Could this be a starting point for an activity this summer?

Step 2: Recollections

Most parents consciously and unconsciously try to structure their children's middle childhood to give them what they most appreciated when they were kids. When planning for summer, parents are especially eager to avoid what they remember as their own parents' errors or disasters. Remembering your own childhood summers will help you understand your child's perspective, but it should also make you think about your own child-rearing practices and how they should affect your child's summer plans.

You probably can't remember much about the years before you were six or seven years old. From then on, however, most adults remember quite a bit. They can tell dozens of stories, rich in detail, about what they did—played cops and robbers with neighborhood friends, made a doll house, had an ice-cream party, picked and canned blueberries, sold lemonade, played baseball in the town Little League, or rode a bike every afternoon for hours. Others talk about where they lived, what they liked, and what was awful. For most adults whose childhoods were reasonably happy, their memories of middle childhood—ages six to twelve—are notable for their variety, humor, and precision.

The following questions will help you remember summers during your middle childhood; you might enjoy sharing the answers with your children.

Remembering Your Summer During Middle Childhood

1. What did you like to do best during the summer? What are your fondest memories of your summers?
2. What did you dislike the most about your summers?
3. Are there activities that you enjoyed during the summer that you still enjoy today? What are they?

4. Who got you started in those activities? When? If you hadn't gotten started in them at that age, do you think you would be pursuing them today?

5. What important gifts or messages did your parents or other adults give you during the summer?

6. Did you have a favorite place to go? Where was it? How did you get there? What did you do there?

7. Have your childhood summer experiences influenced how you raised your own children?

Step 3: Conversations—Listen To Your Child

Listen to your child. Concentrate on what he is *really* saying, and you'll have more clues to his true interests. Feel free to direct conversations by asking your kid up front what he is interested in. The following charts should give you some information to mull over, and help you understand the way your child thinks and what he wants. Take notes about these conversations; no one can rely completely on memory.

When looking over your notes, ask yourself: What is my child telling me? What is my child most curious about now? What might my child want me to know more about?

"What's Fun? What's Fabulous for Summer?" is a list of questions to ask your child. These questions can help you zero in on the areas that most interest your child. They also help you search for resources.

Ask these questions when you're both relaxed. Let your child talk freely; try not to answer the questions for him. One word of caution: Don't decide that you are going to ask all the questions at once. Ask two or three of them at one time and another two or three a few days later.

Listen patiently to your child's answers. Resist feeling overwhelmed, depressed, or discouraged by your child's candor. Avoid the temptation to interrupt and expound on what his interests should be or what he should do. Remember, children vary in ability and age, and this makes a difference in the way they answer questions.

What's Fun? What's Fabulous for Summer?

1. If you could do anything this summer, what would you do? Describe it.
2. What is your favorite thing to do in the summer?
3. Would you like to go to camp? A day camp or a sleepover camp? Why?
4. Would you like to do things around the community? What? Why?
5. Are there places you would like to go to this summer? Where? Why?
6. What are some things your friends do in the summer? Do you wish you could do them too?
7. What do you like doing at the playground? What do you hate?
8. Would you prefer doing something with a friend, or by yourself?
9. What are you good at? What do you think you are not so good at?
10. What do you wish you were better at?
11. What do you wish you could do that you don't know how to do?
12. What do you like to do with the family? Where would you like to go with the family?
13. What did you do last summer that you want to do again this summer? What don't you want to do?
14. What is your best time of day in the summer? Why?
15. What is your worst time of day in the summer? Why?

TRUST YOUR INTUITION: YOU KNOW YOUR CHILD BEST

The *Yes, No, Maybe Summer Chart* is a list of things that children this age do. Filling out this chart gives kids new ideas and shows parents what they are really interested in doing. Kids like putting stick-on dots beside the activities they would really like to try. Those who don't read well will need help, though older kids can fill out the chart by themselves. Many kids, especially young ones, want to do absolutely everything and will check boxes until they run out of chart, which is fun but defeats the purpose. This can be prevented by working on the chart with your child over a period of time so that you can see what is really important to her. You'll probably have to tell her to choose only one or two activities for the summer.

If the chart is too extensive for you to manage, try making your own list, including only resources that you know are available in your community and affordable for your family. For example, if your child is interested in birds, you can respond to this interest in a variety of ways: Help your child use binoculars to study birds, sign her up for an organized bird-watching class, visit the library to check out books about birds, or go to a pet store that carries a variety of birds. You could involve the rest of the family in the interest by going on nature walks, or look into day or sleepover camps that offer hiking, mountain-climbing, or environmental studies.

Remember to share your insights with sitters and other adults who are involved with your child. When they understand what your child is especially interested in doing, they can help support those interests.

You'll want to look at the "Yes" answers first, but the "Maybe" answers can be most revealing in some cases. The challenge is to look at a child's "Maybe" selections to see if there is a cluster of items that relate to one another. A child who checks "Maybe" for the following topics: go on nature walks, look at stars, learn more about whales and endangered animals, make things with shells, and collect rocks and fossils might find nature studies a perfect match.

Yes, No, Maybe Summer Chart

1. Athletic Activities

	YES	NO	MAYBE		YES	NO	MAYBE
Aerobics				Jumping rope			
Archery				Karate			
Badminton				Kayaking			
Baseball, softball				Kite flying			
Basketball				Mountain climbing			
Baton twirling				Paddle boating			
Bicycling				Paddle tennis			
Boating				Pool			
Bowling				Racquetball			
Canoeing				Rollerblading			
Croquet				Roller skating			
Darts				Sailing			
Fencing				Self-defense			
Field hockey				Skateboarding			
Fishing				Soccer			
Football				Street hockey			
Frisbee				Surfing			
Golf				Swimming			
Gymnastics				Tai Chi			
Hiking				Tennis			
Horseback riding				Track and field			
Horseshoes				Water games			
Jogging				Water skiing, water sliding			
Judo				Wrestling			
Juggling				Yoga			

2. Cultural Activities

	YES	NO	MAYBE		YES	NO	MAYBE
ARTS AND CRAFTS				Ceramics			
Airplanes and flying things				Computer graphics			
Architectural design				Crochet			
Batik				Decoupage (collage)			
Cake decorating				Designing, making posters			
Calligraphy				Doll and dollhouse making			
Candle making				Doodle art			
Carpentry				Dough art			
Cartoon drawing				Embroidery			

	YES	NO	MAYBE		YES	NO	MAYBE
Freeehand drawing				*DRAMA*			
Game making				Choral reading			
Illustrating stories				Clown lessons			
Kaleidescope making				Community theater			
Kite making				Costuming			
Knitting				Face painting			
Macrame				Improvisation			
Mask making				Magic tricks and card tricks			
Mathematical art				Make-up workshop			
Model building				Mask making			
Mural painting				Mime			
Needlepoint				Mysteries, creating, reading			
Oil painting				Play production			
Origami				Play writing			
Papermaking and marbling				Prop making			
Photography and light				Puppetry and puppetmaking			
Pottery				Set construction			
Print making				Storytelling			
Puppet making				Theater games			
Puzzle making				Ventriloquism			
Quilting				*MUSIC*			
Rug making				Band			
Sand sculpting				Chamber music			
Sculpting				Chorus			
Sewing				Making instruments			
Stamping with rubber stamps				Song writing			
Tie-dyeing				Voice lessons			
Watercolor				*MUSICAL INSTRUMENT LESSONS*			
Weaving				accordion			
Woodcraft and woodwork				autoharp			
DANCE				cello			
Ballet				clarinet			
Ballroom dance				cornet			
Belly dance				cymbals			
Creative movement				drums			
Folk dancing				flute			
Jazz dance				gong			
Modern dance				guitar			
Square dance				harmonica			
Swing dance				maracas			
Tap dance							

	YES	NO	MAYBE		YES	NO	MAYBE
oboe				triangle			
organ				trombone			
piano				trumpet			
piccolo				tuba			
recorder				viola			
saxophone				violin			
tambourine				xylophone			

3. Community Activities

	YES	NO	MAYBE
American National Red Cross Programs			
Big Brother/Big Sister Association			
Boys' Clubs and Girls' Clubs of America			
Boy Scouts and Girl Scouts of America			
Camp Fire, Inc.			
Collectors' clubs			
Community newspaper			
Computer clubs			
Educational groups (study of mammals, study of rocks)			
4-H programs			
Garden and horticultural groups			
Get a job (care for another person, sell baked goods and candy)			
Historical societies			
Hobby clubs			
Humane Society (taking care of animals)			
Language clubs (French, Spanish, Italian, German)			
Library and reading clubs			
Park and recreation program			
Religious Activities			
Special needs organizations (gifted, handicapped, etc.)			
Sports/fitness programs			
Student letter exchange (pen pals in another country)			
Summer theater groups			
Town, recreation, and community programs			
Volunteer programs			
Writing clubs			
YMCA and YWCA			

4. Outdoor and Nature Activities

	YES	NO	MAYBE
Animal farm or shelter—study the animals			
Archaeological program—attend and participate in a dig			
Astronomy—learn about the universe			
Audubon societies—join in a summer program or go on walks			
Backpacking—go on an adventure			
Beach—walking, building sand castles, and studying marine life			
Bird-watching			
Botanical gardens—explore and study			
Build a birdfeeder—record the birds			
Butterflies—observe, or catch and classify			
Cranberry bog or blueberry farm—visit and study the process			
Farm—visit a few and compare the activities			
Geology—collect, identify, and polish rocks			
Historical sights and neighborhoods—take a walking tour			
Islands—visit one, study life on it, and sleep overnight			
Life on a river—study it			
Mountain climbing			
Natural history—join a club			
Nature centers—attend a local program and crafts class			
Plant a garden—flower or vegetable			
Pond life—explore it			
Science—attend classes and workshops at museums and Planetaria			
Trees, shrubs, and flowers—study and classify			
Whale watching—go on an expedition and learn about whales			
Wild edible plants—study and classify			
Zoo—visit and study the animals			

5. Ideas to Spark Summer Interests

	YES	NO	MAYBE
Animals—adopt and care for one			
Archaeology—go for a dig			
Astrology—study the stars, moon, and sun			
Aviation—learn about planes and make flying things			
Bubbles—make a mixture and experiment			
Cars—learn about old and new models			
C.B. radio			
Chemistry—begin to experiment			
Collecting—baseball cards, coins, dolls, railroad cars, and stamps			
Computers—learn LOGO or BASIC or a graphics program			
Cooking and nutrition			
Designing and writing—ad copy, greeting cards, logos, and gift wrappings			
Entomology—study insects			
Experimenting with electricity			
Film—make home movies			
Finance—set up a bank account and keep track of spending			
Game making—create a board game or a card game			
Game playing—backgammon, billiards, card games, checkers, chess, Clue, cribbage, designing code games, and Dungeons and Dragons			
Genealogy—study your family history or make a tree			
Geography—buy a map of your state and use it			
History—study a period you're interested in			
Humor—write jokes, tell riddles, and read and draw comics			
Inventions—make new things with objects, have a fair			
Journalism—write newspaper stores, ad copy, and press releases			
Languages—learn Spanish, French, Italian, Greek, German, etc.			
Learn about different countries			
Magic—practice tricks and perform shows			
Make a terrarium			
Make treats—candy with molds, ice cream, cookies, no-bake snacks			
Math games—solve math problems			
Mind-stretchers and mind games			
Model car and plane construction			
Navigation—map out the next trip			
Outer space and UFOs			
Pets—training and grooming			
Plant a garden—vegetable, flowers, or herbs			
Protect your environment—recycle at home			
Puzzles—complete 500 or 1,000 pieces and frame			
Radio—short wave and Morse code			

	YES	NO	MAYBE
Radio announcing, taping interviews, and doing productions			
Read books of your choice and keep a record of them			
Research your town and its activities			
Sea and ocean life—learn all about various fish			
Take a "transportation" ride just for fun—train, boat, plane			
Videos—make one			
Write (books, newspapers, poems, plays, and folk tales)			

6. Fun Places to Go in the Summer

	YES	NO	MAYBE		YES	NO	MAYBE
Aquarium				Movies			
Bakery				Museums			
Band concert				Music concert			
Beach				Nature reserve			
Book publisher				Newspaper publisher			
Bottling company				Parades			
Candy factory				Parents' place of work			
Car manufacturing plant				Parks (bring a picnic)			
Cereal factory				Planetarium			
Circus				Political rally			
Clothing manufacturer				Printing company			
Computer company or store				Puppet show			
Country fair				Radio or TV station			
Courthouse or state capitol				River			
Farmers' market				Sports event			
Fireworks display				Sugar factory			
Greenhouse				Telephone company			
Historical site				Theater or summer stock			
Hotel				Top of the highest building			
Lake				Toy manufacturer			
Library				Trip to a relative's home			

Step 4: Watch and Observe

What your child likes to do in his spare time often gives you good clues about his interests. What games does he play? What outdoor toy is always out of the closet? Where does he like to go? Certain materials, equipment, and experiences have meaning for each child. By carefully watching your child at play and at work, you can come up with even more ideas for summer.

Some recent theories on *multiple intelligences* may have implications for what your child learns out of school. One theory proposes that humans have developed intelligence in seven relatively autonomous areas. The areas are logical-mathematical (scientists, mathematicians), linguistic (poets, journalists), musical (composers, violinists), spatial (navigators, sculptors), bodily-kinesthetic (dancers, athletes), interpersonal (therapists, salespeople), and intrapersonal (people with detailed, accurate self-knowledge).

EXPLORE
SUMMER FUN
WITH YOUR CHILD

With that in mind, think about the sorts of things that interest your child. Does he like using poster paints, crayons, or clay? Does he love backpacking, baseball, basketball, bicycling, or boating? Is he crazy about computers, drama, fishing, gymnastics, hiking, horseback riding, mountain climbing, music, sailing, tennis, or swimming? What sorts of games does your child play? Is he curious about musical instruments, cameras, telescopes, binoculars, thermometers, or microscopes? Does he enjoy browsing in book stores, hobby shops, music stores, hardware shops, sporting-goods stores, or cooking stores? What does your child watch on television? What kinds of movies or videos does he like? Does he enjoy going to a particular museum, sporting event, or dance recital? When your child pretends, who or what does he pretend to be? Does he have any special needs that should be considered?

Over a period of time, ask your child to draw a series of pictures or create collages showing the things that he would like to do this summer. Watch what your child likes to draw and create from pictures in magazines and catalogs. As your child cuts out these pictures, have him put together the ones that are of greatest interest. One child might put together seascapes and swim gear, another might gather hundreds of animals, and yet another might assemble a collection of cars. It's fun for children to cut out and glue together their favorite things to do.

Over the next few days, observe your child and list the specific materials, equipment, experiences, or tools that interest him. These unspoken affinities explain a great deal about your child's likes. Consider jotting the information down and putting it in your folder. Regardless of what happens this summer, watching your child like this will teach you more about him.

Step 5: Turn Summer Interests Into Actions— Make Decisions

It's tempting to hope that a perfect plan for your child's summer will just happen. It won't—parents and children *do* need to make decisions. As you sift through your notes, charts, and questionnaires, a few ideas will stand out as strong possibilities for summer activities.

When it comes time to make the final decisions, be sure that your decisions are your own—don't lose sight of your family's values or style of child-rearing. Time and money may be concerns; consider what any plans will require of you before making a firm commitment.

Supporting your child's interests doesn't mean selling the family home and moving in with a world-famous gymnastics instructor. You can find an organization, a club, program, or youth group for nearly every interest imaginable. If your child wants to try woodworking, calligraphy, or chess, look for a group of like-minded people in your area.

Turn Summer Interests Into Actions—Make Decisions

1. What makes sense for my child to do this summer?
2. What are our limits and constraints this summer?
3. What do I want for my child this summer?
4. What should we try to do? Why? For how long?
5. What rules should we make?
6. What kinds of vacations or excursions should we try to go on? Who should go? Why?
7. Whom do we want to see? Why?
8. What do we want to try to guard against?
9. How do these interests fit in with the rest of the family's interests and plans?

Step 6: Expand Your Child's Summer Interests

To expand on summer interests, start where you are—both literally, in your own home and community, and figuratively, in your child's interests and in yours. Then the activity can grow naturally and lead in new directions. Let your child get involved in collecting as much information as she can about topics that interest her. Encourage her to call around and learn about available resources, get addresses, and find out what times places are open. Libraries, tourist bureaus, the yellow pages, and lists of museums or organizations are a few good places to start.

Begin with your child's burning interests and build activities around them. Several days before a beach trip, for example, your child can go to the library and get books on the ocean, marine life, and arts and crafts using shells. While at the beach, everyone can use what they learned to have a better time, and when you get home your child can build on the experience by using shells to make mobiles, jewelry, or ornaments. Your child might decide to write or tape a story called "My Day at the Beach."

When looking for ways to expand on interests, don't overwhelm your child with enthusiasm. Ask questions and give advice that will point her in new directions, but don't drag her along to antique shows or art museums to foster an interest that simply isn't there. The following questions can help you and your child get started.

Ways To Expand a Child's Summer Interests

1. What kind of information does the library or museum have?
2. Are there games to go to or amateur leagues to join?
3. What performances, demonstrations, or lectures could we go to?
4. Can the whole family participate in some related activities?
5. Could we write to companies, groups, or clubs for information or freebies?
6. Are there things to make, create, and build around the interest?
7. What sort of creative things could expand the interest? How about puzzles, board games, and writing projects?

8. Are there any contests related to the interest? Are there any books that might give us more ideas about this?

9. Are there children or adults who live nearby and have the same interests? Are there groups to join?

Eight-year-old Elaine loved animals and was always talking about pandas, dolphins, foxes, seals, elephants, lions and tigers and bears, oh my! She knew all about endangered species and was interested in dinosaurs. Here are some things Elaine's family could do with her:

- Go to the library and get books about one of Elaine's favorite animals each week. She could read about what each animal ate, where and how it lived, and how it seemed to feel about humans.
- Subscribe to magazines such as *National Geographic World*.
- Visit all of the nearby zoos, aquariums, animal farms, and natural history museums.
- Collect posters and pictures of Elaine's favorite animals.
- Make animal cookies and animal puppets.
- Collect stuffed animals and make elaborate homes for them.
- Write to preservation groups such as the World Wildlife Foundation.
- Watch TV programs like Wild Kingdom or Jacques Cousteau.

☆ ☆ ☆

☆ ☆ ☆

Brian loved baseball cards, and whenever he went to the store he tried to convince his parents, sisters, aunt, cousins, or sitter to buy him some. He could quote facts and figures about many of the players and was always interested in talking or playing baseball with anyone who knew the game. Over the summer, Brian and his brother could:

• Visit the Baseball Hall of Fame in Cooperstown, New York.

• Go to baseball games.

• Go to baseball card shows and talk to collectors.

• Write to players' fan clubs.

• Ask local coaches how statistics are taken.

• Join a Little League team.

☆ ☆ ☆

Striking The Delicate Balance

This book offers you a number of choices. Please don't think you have failed as a parent if you don't fill out every list, complete every chart, and produce an award-winning video of your child's summer. What is right for some families may not be for others, and you need to choose activities your family can enjoy without putting pressure on anyone.

As you start thinking about your child's summer, the dreaded specter of the "pushy parent" will probably arise. Are you expecting too much? Because summer activities are essentially optional, you might feel that forcing your kid to practice her piano or go play baseball in the park makes you "pushy," and that being pushy is deplorable. On the other hand, you should sense that your child needs encouragement and support, and sometimes just a little "pushiness." There is a certain wisdom in one father's remark about his children's reluctance to attend a weekly ballet class: "They don't want to go. But they want to be made to go."

If you're nervous about making decisions for your child, take heart—many adults look back on decisive parents with gratitude. When Bill, now a skilled carpenter, reminisces about being an Eagle Scout, he says, "I could have never gotten that badge without my mother. She helped me stick to it all these years."

Beware of becoming too wrapped up in a child's accomplishments, misreading your child's disposition, or encouraging accomplishments that create problems for your child. There is no easy way to find the right balance, but the six steps described before have helped many families. Sometimes, parents just have an intuitive sense that "enough is enough," or "this is really too much."

Children *do* need free time to play during the summer. Play, by definition, is spontaneous and child-initiated. An ideal summer calendar will give a child time to relax a little and still be involved in interesting activities over the summer. Your child needs your help, guidance, and support in deciding what to do and when to do it. Overbooked and overextended children will be unhappy, bored, and uncreative.

Often, children are timid about experimenting and parents have to encourage them to try new activities and follow through. Sometimes parents are accused of being too pushy when they're really responding sensitively to a particular child's temperament. When asked how she fostered her children's abilities, Priscilla, a mother of five, said, "I waited until an interest bubbled up; then I pounced on it. I tried to demonstrate my sensitivity by waiting for each child to give a lead, and then I showed my love for them by following through on those interests."

Searching For the Soul of Summer

Searching For Summer Resources

Every stage of child-rearing leads parents into new territory, but middle childhood is an especially exciting period. Your child's curiosity and newfound interests will have you experiencing your community as if for the first time—entering buildings you've walked by for years, reading parts of the newspaper you'd always skipped, making new friends and new connections. Try going to a Greek grocery store, attending a summer jazz concert, eating dim sum on a Sunday morning, or exploring an antique engine show with your kids. New experiences expand a child's knowledge and appreciation of the world, and parents often have as much fun as their kids do.

Here is a partial list of resources that can help your child explore summer interests, formally and informally: trips, programs, camp counselors, relatives, sitters, coaches, and friends. With your help, your child can find out what she wants to do and how she's going to do it— and be well on her way to a summer of exploration.

Before you start actually looking for summer resources, you should narrow down your choices. At this stage, your family's limits are the most important factor. Eliminate all camps or programs that you can't afford and any activity that entails transportation problems or asks parents to give more time than you could handle. And, of course, decide if any kinds of programs would be inconsistent with your family values.

Here are some ideas for learning about summer options:

MAKE YOUR NEIGHBORHOOD AN EXCITING PLACE TO VISIT

✔ Look up all the resources in your community that might be summer-oriented. Talk to teachers, principals, counselors, or members of youth-serving organizations.

✔ Ask your child what he especially enjoyed doing last summer. Suppose he describes the great time he had examining his friend's kite collection or watching a hockey game. Have a friend who travels bring back foreign currency or look into hockey programs in the area.

✔ Talk to other children about what they did last summer. Ask them what was good about their summer and what was bad about it.

✔ Ask if children's programs are offered at the museums, zoos, churches and religious groups, or national or state parks in your area during the summer.

✔ Find out if your local pool or lake offers a children's swimming program or has designated children's swimming hours with a lifeguard on duty.

✔ Learn what programs and activities your local parks and recreation department offers for children during the summer.

✔ Consider getting together with several other families to hire a sitter, artist, coach, or other instructor to work with a group.

✔ Find out if youth organizations such as 4-H, American National Red Cross, Big Brothers/Big Sisters, the Ys, Scouts, Boys' and Girls' Clubs, or Camp Fire offer summer programs.

✔ See if your local PTA maintains a file of parents' and children's responses to past summer programs.

✔ Compile a list of possible summer camps; the local library, school or PTA, municipal park, or church may have some suggestions. Also, ask other parents for their recommendations. Your options may include day camps and overnight camps; general camps offering arts and crafts, sports, swimming, camping, and drama; and specialized camps that focus on one main activity (like hockey, tennis, computers, or French) while providing the general camp experience of canoeing and cookouts. Summer camps vary greatly in price, quality, duration, distance from home, and number of participants. Ask lots of questions and investigate all the options.

✔ Read about camps. For example, the American Camping Association (ACA) publishes a *Guide to Accredited Camps* every year. Peterson's annual *Summer Opportunities for Kids and Teenagers* is another useful resource.

✔ Attend a camp fair sponsored by the ACA. Fairs are held all over the country, and the *Guide to Accredited Camps* lists phone numbers for local contacts.

✔ Look into camp referral services—consultants and companies that provide information and will help you get in touch with camp directors. Ask plenty of questions before using such a service, as well as before enrolling your child in any camp.

✔ If you live near a city or plan to visit one, check if there is a parents' paper that offers information on events for families. Collect and save these. Call local newspapers or look in the classifieds. Books like *In and Out of Boston with (or without) Children* (Bernice Chesler, Globe Pequot Press) are available for most major cities.

✔ Learn whether your library offers any summer programs for children, such as reading groups or film series.

✔ Ask your child's teacher for a recommended summer reading list.

✔ Call your local child-care resource and referral offices. Find out if they have information on programs.

✔ Ask your employer about services for working parents.

✔ Think about a vacation or excursion your child might take to visit a friend or relative in another city by train or bus.

✔ Consider a family vacation that is as fun and carefree as possible, includes something that everyone likes to do, and eliminates everyday hassles. Avoid long drives!

✔ Plan a few day trips that are somewhat out of the ordinary.

✔ Ask the parents of your child's friends if they would be interested in planning activities or excursions with you. In one case, five couples chipped in and hired an assistant to work with their children all summer. Each parent then took charge for a week, organizing activities for the group. One father who was a veterinarian took the kids to the zoo, to pet stores, and to an animal hospital. When it rained they watched *Lady and the Tramp* and made collages.

Gathering and Sorting Ideas

When gathering summer resources, get as many leads as you can—names, addresses, and phone numbers of organizations, institutions, and people. Most of the leads you follow will bring you to a few more names and numbers. As you network, you'll probably be surprised at how many resources there really are for children, even in small towns.

Write down everything you learn by talking to people, surveying the neighborhood, making phone calls, and writing letters. These notes and any notes you've kept on your child's interests will be invaluable when you're making final decisions about summer programs.

Once you have a list of possible contacts, you can start narrowing it down by calling or writing for more information. You'll need to set aside a block of time to make your initial calls and write your letters. If you don't have that kind of free time, try splitting up the calls over several days, or enlist the help of an articulate friend. Be persistent and keep calling or writing until you get all the information you need.

Telephone Exploration Sheet for Summer

Activity/Organization/Camp _____

Telephone Number _____

Contact Person _____

Brief Description _____

Ages _____

Cost _____

How Long _____

Starting Date _____

General Impressions _____

Issues Important To Our Family _____

_____

"Things used to be so simple," is a refrain often heard by almost every child. Indeed, our grandchildren will probably be forced to hear how we had to walk uphill both ways in the snow to the one-room schoolhouse, back when life was simpler and better. The nugget of truth here is that things are generally more complicated than they used to be; by the time you get done tracking down your leads and compiling your information, you'll probably be willing to agree.

Organizing the phone numbers, times, dates, costs, and names which will lead to summer fun is hard work. Your family should consider a number of questions about any program, camp, or trip, as well as about your resources, before making final decisions. Asking yourself these questions will help you and your child find the best summer plan—the one that she'll love and grow with; the one that won't drive you crazy.

The first step is to ask questions of yourself as a parent. You must answer honestly—at least to yourself—before you can make realistic summer plans for your child.

Start by considering time and money. Family trips and summer camps involve a one-time commitment of each, but you should still look into scholarship programs, transportation costs, and possible equipment rental or purchase. Ask questions like, "If I cancel, will I get a refund?" Community programs, on the other hand, require a sustained commitment. How many sessions will you have to pay for in advance? Are parents ever required to participate? What are the projected costs of continuing the program for two years? Who will drive the child to and from the activity?

Once you've answered those questions, you need to look at specific programs and instructors or directors. Ask program directors questions like: What kind of experience do you have? What do others say about your skills? How is progress reported back to parents?

Furthermore, you need to ask about the nature of the program itself: Is it part of a series? Is there another level, and what's involved in it? Does the group sponsor any events during the school year?

You should also learn who your child will be with in the camp or program. This means knowing about the ages, sexes, and experience levels of other children in the program. If your child has friends in the program, or if other kids live close by, you should look into a way of sharing transportation costs.

Call early. Camps have specific schedules and application deadlines. Programs in your community might fill up quickly, especially if they're inexpensive. Camping grounds might also be full if you wait too long, so don't hesitate to make final decisions, especially about camps.

Financial aid for many summer camps and programs is typically limited and not well-advertised, so ask about it specifically if your family needs assistance. Sports equipment can often be found at thrift stores, or when schools and organizations have equipment exchanges. Look for music stores that rent instruments, and check the want ads for second-hand recreational equipment. (Camps often provide equipment, so your camp-bound kid may need little more than her clothes and a toothbrush.) Look into special deals on travel and accommodations.

Above all, be flexible. When investigating community resources, you are likely to find surprises just around the corner. When planning trips, be aware that what you are planning to see or do may not be the most exciting thing to see or do when you get there. Take advantage of unsolicited opportunities.

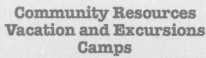

Community Resources
Vacation and Excursions
Camps
Summer Interests / Places to Visit

WHEN?
How often does it meet?
What is the schedule?
Are missed classes a problem?
Are there make-up sessions?
When am I required to be there?

WHERE?
Where is it offered?
Can one get there by public transit or car pool?
How far is it from home?

COST
What is the fee?
Do we pay by the week or by month?
Is there a scholarship program?
If we cancel do we get a refund?
How many sessions must we pay for initially?
Must we buy or rent any equipment?

WHO INSTRUCTS?
Who are the counselors?
Who is the instructor?
How much experience has the instructor had?
What do other people say about this person's skills?
How will progress be reported to parents?

WHO ELSE DOES IT?
What are the ages, sexes, and experience levels of the others signed up?
Who will my child know?
Is it possible to contact other families to work out car pools?

WHAT ELSE?
How structured is this program?
Is it part of a series?
Is there another level and what's involved in it?
Do you sponsor any free or special summer events?

Resources That Promise the Best Summer Yet

If you've reached the point where you have all your information, everyone has written back, and you have notebooks chock-full of interesting information, congratulations. But don't put your feet up just yet—you need to sort through what you've found and decide what your family's options are.

Summer resources outside the home can be divided into three groups: community programs, trips, and camps. You and your child will almost certainly end up deciding on a balance of these three, perhaps selecting one to concentrate on, or building a summer made up of equal parts of each.

Community Programs

Of the three, activities near the home—using community resources and park programs—are often the easiest to find out about. In addition, you will probably be able to get personal recommendations from friends, or fellow parents about the best instructors and programs. Your child will probably be home for at least part of the summer, and community programs can help to fill up empty days.

Unfortunately, some communities have limited resources, and you may have only one or two options. You should still look into each program carefully. Some organizations have good reputations; others do not. You need to make sure that the activity you and your child choose together is right for everyone involved.

Groups of parents can hire teachers and coaches to teach gymnastics, swimming, flute—whatever it is their children have shown a genuine interest in pursuing. The right instructor will nurture that interest, help children develop their skills, and encourage them to excel.

Instructors, Artists, or Musicians

When choosing an instructor, first look for expertise. Who teaches flute? Ask people. Where is the best place to learn macramé or photography? Next, look for people with knowledge of children and a love of teaching.

Try to assess a candidate's reliability, knowledge of the field, and rapport with children. Is he or she enthusiastic, flexible, and engaging enough to get the child going? Fairly dependable about keeping appointments? Does he or she seem to develop a sense of camaraderie and respect between all involved? More specifically, you might ask artists how they would teach art to children this age. What kind of art projects would they recommend? Do they feel the process or product is more important?

Suggestions for Interviewing Instructors, Artists, or Musicians

1. What are the age, physical, and reading requirements for taking these lessons?
2. What do you see as your expertise in helping children this age to learn?
3. Do you expect the children to practice in the summer? If so, how much? Why?
4. What expectations do you think we could realistically establish for children over the summer?
5. Do you have any ideas on how to keep a child's interest alive?
6. Do you teach individual or group lessons? How many children are likely to be in a group?
7. What kind of children most benefit from taking these lessons?
8. How long have you been teaching _____? Can you tell me/us a little about your background and qualifications?
9. Can you provide the names and phone numbers of two families for whom you have already worked?
10. How do you teach?
11. What other skills and abilities might a child develop by participating in this endeavor?
12. What is your summer schedule like? How often would you recommend lessons?
13. Do you have any suggestions for parents as to how they could support this interest at home?

Coaches

Coaches can have a lot of influence on your child during these years. If parents are hiring a coach to work with a group of children, they should interview that person thoroughly. If you're arranging for your child to participate in community-sponsored sports, you have little, if any, choice about coaches, but you can still evaluate them by watching practices or games. A coach's reaction to frustrations and setbacks, such as comments made to individual players after an easy victory or a tough loss, should give you an idea of what to expect.

Make sure the coach is right for your child. How does the coach feel about girls' participation in group sports? What are his or her attitudes about winning and losing?

Suggestions for Interviewing Coaches

1. How are you trained and certified in this sport?
2. During the summer, how many games are there? How many practices?
3. Are you interested in working with a small group of children in our community? Do you have the time available? When?
4. What time of day and how long is each game or practice session?
5. What kind of child most benefits from being involved?
6. What are the costs of the various aspects (travel, equipment, etc.)?
7. How do you encourage good sportsmanship among players? (Does the coach appear to be a positive role model?)
8. Are your expectations different for boys and girls? If so, how?
9. How do you determine who will be on the starting team?
10. How do you decide how long each child will play?
11. How important is it to have a winning team?
12. What do you do to help further the growth of a "natural athlete" or an "uncoordinated" child?
13. How do you ensure safe playing conditions?
14. Are there any hazards particular to this sport? How are you trained to handle emergency procedures, first aid, etc.?
15. Do you provide nutritional counseling if it's important for participation in the sport?

Sitters

Sitters should be reliable and energetic. You want someone who can take your child to a swimming lesson or ride the bus with him to shop for a birthday present. Take into account your child's age, maturity, and temperament when hiring a sitter. If you're not sure whether you need a sitter, ask yourself how safe your neighborhood is, and how many hours your child will spend home alone.

Six- to twelve-year-olds can get along with almost any type of sitter. Don't limit your choices—think about males or females, younger or older people, or people whose cultural or ethnic background your child might find interesting. Look for a sitter whose interests could intrigue your child. Does the person know batik or kite-making? Sailing and swimming? Hire a sitter who has an expertise and a desire to share it with your child.

Suggestions for Interviewing Sitters

WHAT ACTIVITIES DID YOUR CHILD ENJOY DOING WITH OTHERS LAST SUMMER?

1. I/we need a sitter to care for___children, ages___, for___hours each week. The pay is___per hour. Are you interested in this job?
2. What is your experience with children this age?
3. Can you provide the names and phone numbers of two families for whom you have already worked?
4. What kinds of activities do you like to do with children?
5. What kinds of activities did you especially enjoy as a child?
6. What are your hobbies and interests? Are you willing to share some of them? What are some of the things you like best?
7. What are some of the ways in which you set limits and discipline children this age?
8. Do you smoke?
9. Do you have a driver's license? Can you help us with transportation? What kind of insurance coverage do you have for your car?
10. What are your career goals?
11. What would you do in an emergency? Do you have any first aid training?

Vacations and Excursions

An occasional change of pace helps your child stay interested and involved in her regular summer activities. From week-long vacations to simple excursions into town, the key word for a family trip in the summertime is *planning*. Planning trips with your kids lets them feel involved and keeps them from pestering you about when you're leaving, when you're coming back, or whether you're almost there.

For some families, a series of short excursions become the highlight of a summer. Other families prefer packing up and going somewhere new and different for a longer stay. Excursions and vacations can be active or laid back, but you need to decide which it will be ahead of time. Combining opportunities for raucous fun with some time for relaxation can give each member of the family a chance to do his or her own thing.

Vacations

The best vacation will be of interest to everyone. Consider each family member's needs, likes, and dislikes. *Great Vacations With Your Kids*, by Dorothy Ann Jordon and Marjorie Adoff Cohen, and *Super Family Vacations*, by Martha Shirk and Nancy Klepper, outline some basic principles for successful family vacations.

- Be sure to plan your vacation with the needs of each family member in mind. Start with the youngest child and work your way up.
- Involve your children in deciding where to go and what to do. Agree on a general level of activity or relaxation.
- Be sure to bring along a few exciting books for everyone to read in the car, train, or plane. Colored string for making friendship bracelets is great, as are travel games and music everyone can sing along to.
- Don't force your child to spend every waking moment with the family. Try finding other kids for them to spend time with (this can be good for your sanity too), have one parent spend time alone with a child, or let children go off under other adult supervision—as many reasonable combinations as you can think of.
- Go where you're wanted. Avoid places that don't welcome young children.
- Plan days around everyone. Kids shouldn't have to spend hours at museums and parents shouldn't have to live at the amusement park.
- Be realistic. You're not going to be able to see and do everything. Remember to be flexible and stay open to new plans. Your vacation's success will be measured in terms of family fun, not family feuds.

A good way to get the whole family involved in vacation planning is to make a chart on which everyone lists how they feel about one activity or another. Then get everyone together and talk about the activities each person prefers and what choice would keep as many family members as possible happy.

Successful trips don't necessarily have to involve the whole family. Brenda, age seven, was uproariously excited about a trip she took to visit her friend Sophia at the beach. "We stayed up all night and talked," Brenda said. "We slept outside in a tent. And we went to this neat penny candy store and they said they wanted me to come back. I want to go back. Oh, I forgot—there were lots of minnows at the beach and we made a huge castle."

Marcy, age twelve, visited New York last summer. "We did everything," she said. "We went to the Empire State Building, the Statue of Liberty, and lots of shops. I could spend the whole day in my favorite toy store in New York. We went back there three times in one day."

☆ ☆ ☆

Suggestions for Family Vacations

- Visit the child's grandparents for a birthday celebration.
- Even if you've never tried any of them before, consider a vacation that involves canoeing, kayaking, hiking, cycling, or white-water rafting.
- Send your child to sleep over at a friend's or sitter's house, or have a sleepover at home, with the whole family camping in one person's room.
- Plan an overnight camping trip to a local campground, or take a longer trip to a national park or nature preserve.
- Visit a lake, mountain range, or beach.
- Go on a cruise or a boat ride.
- Stay at a farm or dude ranch.
- Tour a major city, such as Boston, Washington, or San Francisco, or an historical place like Williamsburg.
- Take a sports-oriented vacation, where everyone can play tennis, golf, sail, or play the sport of their choice.
- Visit an adventure or theme park.

✌ Visit a state or national park. Be sure to call ahead to local tourism bureaus for information.

Excursions

Even one-day excursions give you a nice break from your summer routine and they can be full of discovery, excitement, and surprises. Excursions with other families or groups of friends have an atmosphere of adventure, even if you're only going downtown or for an hour's drive into the country. Summer excursions are your child's passport to new places and different worlds.

Suggestions for Family Excursions

✗ A newspaper to see the newsroom, layout area, and printing presses.

✗ An assembly line to watch cars being made.

✗ An amusement park to try the new water slide.

✗ A toy factory where they make games, trucks, or dolls.

✗ A costume company that stocks outfits for Peter Pan, the Teenage Mutant Ninja Turtles, or the Muppets.

✗ A candy store where chocolate is being melted, molded, wrapped, and packed.

✗ Second-hand shops, auctions, or estate sales to see all sorts of old clothes, books, toys, furniture, and trinkets.

✗ A farm to learn about raising and breeding animals, and planting and harvesting of crops.

✗ A county fair to see the prize animals, fruits, and vegetables.

✗ City Hall to watch the mayor or other city officials at work.

✗ The State Capitol to watch legislators debate, see the Governor's office, and learn how a bill becomes a law.

✗ An experimental station to see how new hybrid varieties of flowers and vegetables are tested and rated.

✗ The post office to watch mail being sorted and weighed. Look for stamp collections that appeal to a variety of interests.

✗ A fish hatchery to see trout or salmon being raised.

✗ Natural wildlife preserves.

- ✗ A U.S. Coast Guard station.
- ✗ A local lake or river for canoeing and hiking. Bring along a picnic lunch.
- ✗ A nuclear or coal power plant in your area to learn how electricity is made.

Camps

Some kids have happy memories of camp and tell wonderful stories about the time they locked a friend out of the cabin or the picnic when the bear nearly ate everyone's sandwiches. Others go on and on about the horrible food, the kids they didn't like, the poison ivy, the time they threw up in their sleeping bag, and how they waited frantically for packages and letters. Missy remembered the time she ate half a sandwich covered in ants before she realized what everyone was laughing about. Making new friends, doing new things, and being on one's own are all important aspects of summer camp.

Different camps appeal to different kids. When choosing a camp, match your child's needs to the program. Be aware that some kids are ready to go to camp earlier than others. The fact that Amadeus Jones down the street is spending the summer at a music program in Germany doesn't mean your Elizabeth is ready to be away from home for an extended period of time. Some children can handle day camps but not sleepover ones.

Generally, camps are either private or agency-sponsored. Private camps are usually owned by individuals or groups, though some are funded by endowments.

Agency-sponsored camps include those run by the YMCA and YWCA, the Girl Scouts or Boy Scouts, or religious organizations like Jewish community centers or Catholic or Protestant churches. Social service agencies often run camps for children with special needs. An agency-sponsored camp has the advantage of a national reputation, and their many locations across the country may make it easier for you to get your child to and from camp.

Specialty camps allow your child to concentrate on a single activity such as hockey, writing, or environmental issues. Cristy wrote her aunt the following letter from space camp:

"Dear Gracie,

Thank you for the baseball cards. Happy Birthday. At Space Camp we got to escperince weightlessness. We also got to go on a mission. A mission was were you could pick a position (I chose principal investigator) and you would be handed a script and you would go on a simulated mission. I was down at Mission Control. Our mission was to launch Space Shuttle Discovery. I have it repair a satellite. We also hung around Kennedy Space center (where we got to see a whole bunch of movies) and visited U.S. Astronaut Hall of Fame.

Love, Cristy."

General camps give campers a wider variety of outdoor experiences. The best way to find a good camp is to ask other parents, check out the latest *Guide to Accredited Camps*, or write to the American Camping Association for information about a specific camp.

If possible, visit a camp you are considering while it is in session. Look at the campers. What sorts of activities are they involved in? What role are counselors playing? Are campers involved in creative work, like building a bird house? Is there a sense of team spirit?

Don't forget to ask for references, watch the counselors interact with campers, ask about counselors' qualifications, assess the physical facilities, and watch the children's faces to get a feel for the camp.

Suggestions for Interviewing Camp Directors

1. How do campers get to the camp? Is there transportation from the bus station, airport, or closest major city to the camp? How much?

2. What is housing like? Are sleeping spaces well-ventilated and comfortable? Do the kids have lockers? Are the bathrooms indoors? Do the cabins have electricity? Where do the counselors stay?

3. How sanitary is the camp? What's the food like? Is the water safe?

4. How do parents keep track of their child's progress?

5. What kind of medical arrangements are provided? Is there a doctor or nurse living at the camp? What happens if an injury occurs away from camp, like on a canoeing trip? Is there a hospital nearby?

6. Who goes to the camp? What is the average age of a camper? What religious and ethnic groups are represented?

7. What kind of leaders will your child have? What is the camper-to-counselor ratio? Are the counselors screened? What references does the camp director have?

8. What is the camp's philosophy? What is its attitude about winning?

9. Does the camp offer scholarships? What about tuition refunds?

10. Can you give me some names of former campers as references?

11. What is the camp's policy on drug and alcohol use?

Creativity, Independence, and Safety at Home

It is just as easy to have a celebrated summer at home as anywhere else. In fact, there are all sorts of lessons to be learned and games to be played right in your own backyard. This chapter is devoted to the things you and your child can do to make any summer at home a wonderful one, from fostering the *other* 3 Rs (resourcefulness, responsibility, and reliability) and being safe, to just having fun and most of all, keeping you from going crazy.

Setting Up Creative Backyard Play Areas

If you have a backyard and a little extra time on your hands, help your child make a fort or a playhouse that can keep her occupied for hours at a time. If you don't have the time, get a high-school student to help out. If the structure is sturdy enough, your child will return to it for weeks. It can become almost a home away from home; a private club-house where she can play imaginatively or retreat from the world.

Sean and his best friend Dan built a fort by putting two refrigerator boxes together. They played in it for several weeks during the summer. They'd take their lunch into the fort and spend hours fixing the place up. "It was a great place," Sean said. "It had a clock, a place to eat and a sign to put up, and we painted it. I wish we had a picture of it. It's gone. Someone broke it down on us and we lost our tools and Dan's watch."

☆ ☆ ☆

Allowing kids to create their own environment lets them discover and explore a world of their own making, one they understand and enjoy. It stimulates their imaginations and, through comparison, lets them better understand the "real world."

Forts and Clubhouses

Building a backyard fort or clubhouse can be as simple as putting two boxes together, or as complicated as you'd like. In one instance, families banded together and helped build five different play areas over a period of ten weeks, giving children chances to play all over the community. Seeing grown-ups cooperate on a project often inspires kids.

Any kid can make a fort out of blankets and a clothesline. If there's an adult around to help, however, consider using tires, buckets, ropes, utility spools, wooden crates, bricks, blocks, boards, barrels, and furniture. Add a fold-up tent to use as a cave or secret hiding place. If you do use any bricks or other potentially dangerous materials, make sure the structure is absolutely safe before letting children play around it.

Obstacle Courses and Outdoor Games

When your children get tired of their fort, most of the materials can be recycled to make an obstacle course. Children love to crawl through barrels, hop over tires, climb ropes, or balance on a board. Check each obstacle for nails or sharp edges before letting your kids run through. Once the course is safe, timing their runs can be a good way to teach them about time and stopwatches.

If there is no time to build a fort, or if no one is interested, you can turn your backyard into a playground by filling an "outdoor box" with balls, beanbags, marbles, jacks, frisbies, chalk, hula hoops, and jump ropes. Be sure to include at least some things that your child can enjoy alone. A football, for instance, won't do much good if there's no one around to catch it. You might want to include a list of outdoor games for groups, including Red Rover, Hide and Seek, all the varieties of Tag, and relay races.

Art and Drama Areas

For some kids, an outdoor art area can inspire all sorts of exciting creative endeavors. Gather chalk, crayons, paper of various colors, different-sized brushes, paints, and materials to make whistles, rattles, and bells, and turn your kid into a young Michelangelo. Expand the art area by adding materials for making mosaics, sculpture, and hand puppets. Outdoors is a good place for messy projects like tie-dying, batik, sand painting, or making sculptures with papier-mâché, soap, or wood.

If your child shows an interest in making hand puppets, make a puppet stage by cutting up a cardboard box and adding some curtains. A group of friends can make up plays and put them on for their families. When the puppet stage gets boring, it can become a fort, a train car, or a castle. Let your child and her friends define and redefine the box until no one remembers exactly what it is and what it has been.

Lemonade Stands and Backyard Wilderness

Lemonade stands have been an American favorite for generations. Get some neighborhood kids together and decide what they want to make and sell (fruit punch, popsicles, slush, bags of snack food). Designing and building the stand fosters creativity, and kids will have a great time making signs and posters advertising their business. When it's all over, a quick rundown of income and expenses could introduce your children to the cruel world of supply and demand.

Coping with a child's demand for adventure, however, shouldn't leave you short on supplies. For example, all you need is a tent (in a pinch, a clothesline, a blanket, and four rocks will do) and a couple of sleeping bags to send your kid and a few friends on a camping trip in your own backyard. Preparations can take a few days as each kid packs, prepares snack food, and makes up a scary ghost story to tell by flashlight. If you're ambitious, you might even want to build a campfire and roast marshmallows.

For more down-to-earth children who don't like the idea of spending a night in the backyard wilderness, creating and maintaining a garden might be a perfect outdoor summer project. A few neighborhood kids can plant, water, and weed flowers or vegetables together. Later in the summer, creating bouquets of flowers or making a special garden vegetable soup or salad for the family gives the project a sense of completion.

Gardeners can make a scarecrow (substitute dry leaves for straw stuffing) to scare birds away, or keep track of plant growth with a chart. Chart-keeping can be as complicated as you'd like. Measuring rainfall or studying lighting conditions gives children an appreciation for the conditions plants need to grow. Kids who don't have a backyard can grow plants in pots on a porch or window ledge. A hint: Radishes grow faster than almost anything, so if your child is anxious for quick results, they may be the most exciting garden choice.

If your child is more interested in building and creating new things than watching them grow, set up an invention area in your backyard. Put together rods, pulleys, and gears, building blocks, and tools so kids can make a weather station, build a small bridge, or create simple machines.

Before you get the idea that a backyard is essential—it's not. Sitters and other adults are sometimes willing to take kids to their houses to play, and neighbors might be willing to share some space. If all else fails, many of the above plans can work on a porch or even on the sidewalk, or at a public park. So take heart, don't despair, just find a small open area—the space will be as interesting and as large as your child's imagination wants it to be.

Rainy Days and Mondays

At some point this summer, you'll wake up ready for the wonderful excursion you had planned (you'll have taken the day off work), look outside at the weather, and feel your heart sink as you realize that a trip to the local lake is no longer a good idea. On other days, the summer doldrums will set in and your child "won't have anything to do." The solution is to plan ahead and always have an idea or two ready to go in case of a bad day. Build the ideas around your child's current interests— a football video for the active type, a new magazine is perfect for the bookish one.

Start a collection. There are a hundred things your child can collect and classify. Help your child start a rock, mineral, coin, stamp, baseball card, plastic dinosaur, or sea life collection. Yard sales and flea markets are often treasure troves of collectibles for a child.

Organize a Fourth of July parade. Help your child plan a neighborhood parade by talking to the local kids and adults. Let the kids make signs announcing the event and have them decorate bikes, carts, or strollers with streamers, kites, balloons, and flags. This is a perfect time to get everyone involved in making balloon animals (with environmentally-safe balloons), bubble-blowing, and playing carnival-type games. Dolls, teddy bears, and pets can also march in the parade. End the parade somewhere that everyone can picnic and play outdoor games.

A RAINY DAY SOLUTION: GET INVOLVED WITH ONE OF YOUR CHILD'S CURRENT INTERESTS

Go star-gazing. Study a map of the universe before you all go outside. Clear, moonless nights are best for star-gazing, and you'll see much better if you get away from lighted homes or cities. A compass and telescope will be useful. Help your child record the constellations you saw, then learn about the myths behind the constellations, describe and draw them (glow-in-the-dark stars to attach to the ceiling are usually a big hit). A good day to do this is July 20, the anniversary of the first Moon landing. Kids can make astronaut puppets, read about the Apollo space missions, and eat "space food."

Explore your city, town, or community. Discuss the various neighborhoods that make up your town. Learn about the restaurants, ice cream shops, and historical sites. Look at old photos of your city, read about its history, and study its water, sewer, and electrical systems. Consider visiting and talking with people like town merchants and civil servants to learn how the city is run. Find a safe place to talk to tourists and find out why people come to visit your community. Wrap up the day by putting questions on index cards and making a trivia game about your town or community. You may want to end up with a family dinner at a local restaurant you've never visited.

Set up a fancy restaurant in your own home. Let the kids make menus, a sign, and placemats with the name of their restaurant. Your kitchen table can be redecorated with a tablecloth and candles. Let the children handle all the safe parts of cooking a meal, serving it, and cleaning up. You can be a snooty customer.

Make different kinds of ice cream. Make your own ice cream and mix in chocolate chips, blueberries, coconut, raspberries, peaches, chopped nuts, strawberries, cookie chunks, or crushed candy bars. To make ice cream at home, you'll need:

4 eggs
1 ¾ cups sugar
1 ½ teaspoon vanilla extract
¼ teaspoon salt
1 cup evaporated milk
1 quart whole milk
1 empty two-pound coffee can with a plastic lid
1-gallon plastic bucket
Mixing spoon
Five pounds of rock salt
3 trays crushed ice

Write the following directions on a sheet of paper and post them on your refrigerator:

1) Beat the eggs in a large bowl. Add the sugar, vanilla, and salt.

2) Add the milk and stir until smooth.

3) Pour the mix into a pitcher and let it chill in the fridge over-night.

4) Pour the mix into the coffee can until it is 1/2 full. Put the lid on the can.

5) Place a layer of ice in the bottom of the bucket. Pour some salt over it.

6) Put the can into the bucket. Pack layers of salt and ice around the can.

7) Don't cover the top with ice. Turn the can around and around in the bucket.

8) As the ice melts, add more ice and salt.

9) Make sure no water gets into the coffee can.

10) Work for about ten minutes. Then, wipe off the plastic lid. Now your ice cream should start to freeze. Keep turning the can until the mixture is frozen.

11) Stir in your favorite topping.

☛ *A great day for this activity is July 23, the anniversary of the invention of the ice cream cone. The ice cream cone was invented in 1904 in St. Louis, Missouri, by a waffle vendor who rolled up his waffles to use as cones.*

Organize a "Junior Olympics." Plan this event so it can be either indoors or outdoors, depending on the weather. Have everyone decide on events, then figure out what equipment you'll need. You can break up into smaller groups, with each group responsible for one event. Events such as Broom Throw, Yard Dash, High Jump, and the Around-the-House Relay are popular. Think about different ribbons or awards for participants.

Adopt a pet. Spark a leaning experience for your child by bringing home any animal, even something as small as a turtle. Read about the pet before it arrives, and work its care and feeding into your summer schedule. Combine this interest with a trip to the zoo (to see tigers and leopards if your pet is a cat, for instance) or aquarium. For younger children, owning a pet can be a transforming experience. Do be sure that your children really want a pet, and are ready to take care of it.

Create a few activity kits. Put certain materials together to turn an ordinary activity into an exceptional one. It helps if the kits are put together in an interesting, inviting way. Possible ideas for kits include: basket weaving, jewelry making, working with gears, a crystal radio set, a weather station, or a detective kit. Make sure the materials you collect take into account your child's age, skills, and interests. Pack up surprise kits to take along on long drives or vacations.

Read and talk about mysteries. The Encyclopedia Brown books are great. Have kids read the stories out loud and try to guess the answers. For older kids, Sherlock Holmes may be a more rewarding choice. Find a passage in one of his stories where Holmes describes someone he's just met. Discuss the assumptions Holmes makes about the person. Was he right?

Celebrate Beatrix Potter's birthday. Have a tea party on July 6 and read aloud to your child to celebrate the author's birthday. Then have your child write and illustrate a short book about your family's pet or some other animal and read it aloud to the family. The book can be made of pieces of paper folded in half, with a piece of construction

paper for a cover. If there is a pet store nearby, go visit and pet the rabbits and other animals.

Put on a magic show. Go to a magic store and get a book on simple magic tricks for your child. Have him practice a presentation with props, and put on a show for the family. Buy a pack of cards and let your child make up his own tricks. Many kids like to make magicians' hats, choose a costume, and make up a silly name for themselves.

Focus on flight. Build a model rocket from a kit. Start early in the morning since making and decorating the rocket will take a few hours. Or build a kite from wood and paper. Make sandwiches in the shapes of planes and test different kinds of paper airplanes. If it's nice enough to go outside, make your own "rocket launcher":

1) Pour equal parts of vinegar and water into an empty plastic soda bottle.

2) Put baking soda in a paper towel and roll the towel up tightly.

3) Attach paper streamers to a cork. Drop the towel into the bottle and put the cork on as tightly as possible. The ingredients will eventually create a harmless gas which will send the cork flying out of the bottle.

To round out the day, rent an exciting flying movie such as *The Rocketeer*, *Top Gun*, or *Radio Flyer*. If you feel these aren't appropriate for your family, good books on flight include *Anne Morrow Lindbergh: Pilot and Poet*, *Amelia's Flying Machine*, and *The Glorious Flight: Across The Channel With Louis Bleriot*.

☞ *National Aviation Day is August 19, celebrating Orville and Wilbur Wright's historic flight in 1903 at Kitty Hawk, North Carolina, and giving you a perfect excuse to focus on flight.*

Becoming Independent

"I know I can do it. I can do it myself." No matter what your child can do independently—tie her shoelaces, ride a bike, make a model or peanut butter sandwich—the key words are "by myself." Summer planning allows you to create situations in your home that will foster independence.

Being independent is one of the most exciting and magical childhood experiences, for both your child *and* you. You can be proud of children who can accomplish things by themselves. As your child generates his own ideas and gets involved in his own projects, he gains more confidence.

You can help your child gain independence by setting realistic goals for him and teaching him to organize his time to reach these goals. Appropriate goals depend on your family's values and heritage.

A word of warning: The goal is *not* extreme independence. For example, asking your kids to be alone all day is too much. Children between six and twelve are not able to exercise that much control over their free time. They simply do not thrive when forced to be independent.

Children who have clearly defined interests and are involved in activities are likely to be resourceful during playtime. When kids are active, parents can relax. No one has to listen to the perpetual cry of, "There's nothing to do! What can I do?"

Here are a few things you can do to help your child become more independent:

- ✔ Organize the house
- ✔ Establish routines
- ✔ Do summer chores together
- ✔ Avoid boredom at home
- ✔ Encourage summer reading
- ✔ Guide television watching

Organizing the House

Physical spaces influence children's behavior. A disorganized house makes your child dependent on you for information. If your child knows where things are, and if the things she needs are within her reach, she can get what she wants, use it, and put it away all by herself.

Suggestions for Organizing Your Home

- Choose one accessible "activity" cabinet to store children's art and game supplies. Include drawing pens, crayons, paints, rubber stamps, construction paper, safety scissors, markers, and glue.
- Keep a realistic and up-to-date list of ideas for your child called "Fun Things to Do When There's Nothing to Do" posted prominently.
- Choose another accessible cabinet to store plastic eating utensils, paper plates, and snack foods. Post a list of no-bake snacks close by.
- Establish a central place for leaving notes and telephone messages.
- Post a list of important phone numbers, including emergency ones—fire, police, and medical.

Establishing Routines

Giving your child routines will help him understand the way time works. Children this age are particularly eager to make sense of time, and will pester you with questions like, "How long until bedtime?" "How soon until school starts?" and "When will we get there?"

Almost every family establishes routines which help its members get things done and provide a sense of security. Most families do this so naturally that their routines are not even visible to outsiders. Generally speaking, however, families that do not actually establish and talk about their organization of time fall into conflict. You can best help your child understand the family's routines by talking to him frequently about the family's plans and how he fits into them. In fact, talking should be part of the routine itself.

Suggestions for Understanding Routines

- Hang a calendar in a prominent place. Decide if you want to set up weekly calendars for each child in his bedroom.
- Have clocks in several rooms. Give children their own watches. Make sure that at least one clock is *non*-digital.
- Ask children to repeat their plans for the day. "Who is meeting you today?" "Which bus are you taking today?"
- Put written reminders in the same place every day. It is not a good idea to leave notes on the front door.
- Make breakfast or dinner regular sharing times for the family.
- Arrange backup systems for when the routine breaks down. Remember, it *will* break down!
- Discuss with your child the ways the routine might break down when you aren't around. Think through solutions together.

Doing Summer Chores Together

If your kid is like most children, chores rank high on her list of most hated things to do. When it comes down to it, chores are probably the cause of more grumbling and family arguments than anything else.

Even so, in most families, everybody pitches in. Families that don't need much help from children still assign their kids age-appropriate tasks and put them in charge of taking care of themselves and their possessions. Giving your kid chores means giving her a certain amount of responsibility; that responsibility, in turn, will help her understand how the family works and how she fits into it.

Suggestions for Getting Your Kids Excited About Chores

- ✘ Identify and list all chores that need to be done, either on a daily or weekly basis. Each member of your family should be assigned chores on the list.

- ✘ Select appropriate chores for each child. Make sure your child is able to do what she's supposed to.

- ✘ Make a creative reminder system that is fun to use and follow. Kids will enjoy chores more if they can keep track of finishing them with stickers or markers. When your child sees how her tasks fit into the family setting, she will feel more in control and less like a victim of other family members' demands.

- ✘ Allow children enough time to complete their chores.

- ✘ Give everyone positive feedback about what they're doing. Frequent praise is enough for some kids, but others would rather get treats in return for the work they do. Try making a coupon book with rewards like a free movie or a trip to the zoo.

- ✘ Don't view children as "free labor." When you see your child watching TV, relaxing in a rocking chair, or reading a book, don't ask her to help out right away. When you interrupt a child's private moments or relaxation time, her response is likely to be one of annoyance, deep pain, or sudden lethargy. When a child is asked to do a chore on demand, the response will probably be, "Not now," or "In a little while, I promise."

Avoiding Boredom at Home

An increasing number of American families are finding that they need to leave children home alone over the summer, especially if both parents work. No child left alone for large blocks of time during the summer will become independent and resourceful. Most children, however, can successfully handle short periods of time alone, especially if you prepare them for it carefully.

This summer, start with very short periods of time—say, about half an hour—while you take a sitter home or run a quick errand. Always give children a clear understanding of how long you will be away and where you will be. If you're going somewhere you can't be reached (like the post office or the grocery store), leave the phone number of a trusted neighbor or relative.

Gradually, your child will be able to handle larger blocks of time alone. The key to success here, as elsewhere, is planning. Make sure your child knows what his choices are during the time he is alone; otherwise, the time will be depressing and lonesome. Make lists of fun things he can do by himself. If you don't, rest assured that the only idea most children will come up with is watching TV. Leaving a laundry list of chores is not helpful—your child will learn to cope with larger blocks of time alone only when given the opportunity to make specific choices.

A little note listing a few options for your child, including a choice of games, will help him feel less alone when you're gone. Consider sending him a fun package from time to time in the mail. Remind him where to find the list of emergency phone numbers, where you are, and when you'll be back. You will be late sometimes; if you can, call ahead to make his wait less stressful.

Periodically, talk with your child about what he did while you were gone and how it felt to be alone. Ask if there was anything that scared, bothered, or concerned him. It is important to evaluate experiences frequently.

Try to do rewarding things on the weekend with your child so he feels good about the accomplishment of staying home alone. Your child needs to hear you say, "I'm so proud of you for staying home alone Tuesday afternoon. You did a good job this week, and you've really grown. I'm also glad you went to the park and played baseball and still came home on time. Good work."

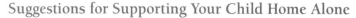

Suggestions for Supporting Your Child Home Alone

1. Be certain your child can follow a routine relatively easily.
2. Watch to see if your child has developed any fears regarding the dark, strangers, or being alone.
3. Help your child read and understand messages and instructions.
4. Listen carefully if your child reports any problems.
5. Ask yourself, "Is he taking on too much responsibility?"
6. Watch closely, and ask yourself, "Do I see any obvious changes in my child's behavior regarding eating habits, friendships, ability to concentrate, seriousness, or sense of humor? Are these indications of trouble?"
7. From time to time, talk about what it's like being home alone. Ask your child what he does when he's alone. Does he usually tell you, "Nothing," or "I was bored"?

Encouraging Summer Reading

For kids, reading to themselves is exhilarating. It creates a sense of independence, because they don't have to wait until you're free to read aloud to them and they can choose their own books, magazines, and comic strips.

Soon after children begin reading to themselves, parents notice a leap ahead in independence.

Being able to read opens the whole world of books to children, but that isn't all. Suddenly, notes from Mom make sense, and so do signs on buildings and streets, and charts and diagrams. Things like telephones, typewriters, and computers make sense for the first time.

Usually, children who read have parents who read. If your child sees you engrossed in a book, magazine, or newspaper, or hears you talking about something you read, he learns that reading is part of growing up. Research shows that the years from ten to twelve are often when a child develops lifelong reading habits. These are also the years when children may have many activities to distract them while reading gets tougher because of smaller print and more abstract concepts.

After making sure your child has access to all sorts of reading material, reading aloud is the best thing you can do to help her read and love books. There is hardly a child who does not respond to being read to. Younger children learn the conventions of reading: how to hold a book, how to turn pages, and how to move sequentially through a story. Older children learn new words and expressions.

Children love picture books, color photos, comic books, and other materials that teach them how to decode pictures. Learning to understand pictures helps kids understand letters and words. Even if you're worried about your child's first choices of reading materials, it is best to let well enough alone. Children's interest in reading is so precious that personal choices must be respected.

Suggestions for Summer Reading

✔ Realize that even seven minutes a day is enough to improve your child's reading. Twenty minutes a day is enough to turn your child into an excellent reader.

✔ Set aside a period of time for parents and children to read aloud.

✔ Post a sheet on your child's bulletin board where she can list each book she reads.

✔ Organize reading materials so children can find what they're looking for.

✔ Shelve books by subject, store magazines together, and keep all reference books in the same place.

✔ Subscribe to one or two magazines for your child. Children love to get mail, and they will read these over and over.

✔ For kids who don't seem to enjoy reading, Asterix and Tintin books are the answer. Parents say these densely illustrated books work like magic for children who are having difficulty.

✔ Send reading "care packages" to children at camp.

✔ Use family trips and excursions as a way of expanding children's reading. Read maps and travel brochures together when planning trips.

✔ Build on friendships made at camp or while on vacation by encouraging children to exchange letters and clippings.

ENCOURAGE
TWENTY MINUTES
OF READING
A DAY

Guiding Television Watching

Children between the ages of six and twelve tend to watch too much TV. The only people who deny this are the kids themselves, who have a vested interest in the matter. To add to your worries, the shows your kids watch are sometimes violent and frightening.

Couch potatoes who watch as much as four or five hours of television a day often show signs of learning problems, restless behavior, and reading deficiencies. These children score lower on achievement tests than children who watch less television. If they are weaned (kicking and screaming) from the television, their test scores and reading levels improve.

How much television viewing goes on in your home? You probably shouldn't let your child watch more than two hours of television a day. The process of setting limits on TV time, especially if your child is alone at home during the summer, is a continuing one.

Limits alone are not enough, however. Simply explaining that TV is bad will not help your child become a critical TV viewer. Talk about television with your child, as he may not understand that some of what he sees isn't real. You need to talk to your child about stereotypes—in terms of race, class, and gender—to make sure he grows up with your family's, not your television's, values.

Also, talking about the difference between TV and books can help your child become less interested in TV and more interested in reading. Make the point that books happen "in your head" while TV doesn't make you think. What would your child change about TV if he could? How could TV be more real?

Before talking to your child about television, consider your own viewing habits. What kind of example are you setting?

Suggestions for Critical Television Viewing

- Read the television guide with your children and decide what shows to watch.
- Create a list of acceptable programs for each child. Update it regularly.

- ✌ Be clear about the amount of TV your kid can watch each day. Guard against a situation where he feels TV time can be saved up.
- ✌ Keep an accurate log of exactly how many hours you and your child watch TV in a week. Decide if you need to limit viewing time.
- ✌ Read aloud to your children instead of letting them watch TV.

Suggestions for Critical Video Watching

- ✔ Limit the time children watch videos the same way you do with television.
- ✔ Try to choose videos appropriate to your child's age. You may want to preview videos before your child watches them, or watch along with your child and discuss the program afterward.
- ✔ Pick videos that will hold your child's attention for repeated viewings. Keep your child's current interests in mind.
- ✔ Look for award-winning videos made specifically for children. Many magazines review children's videos. Look in *Family Circle*, *Parenting*, and *Parents' Choice*.
- ✔ Consider renting these all-time favorites:

All Time Family Favorite Video List

Anne of Green Gables	Short Circuit (I and II)
Beauty and the Beast	Singin' in the Rain
Bye-Bye Birdie	Sleeping Beauty
Captains Courageous	Snoopy Come Home
Charlie and the Chocolate Factory	Spirit of St. Louis
Charlie Brown's All Stars	Star Trek: The Motion Picture
Charlotte's Web	Star Trek II: The Wrath of Khan
Cinderella	Star Trek III: The Search for Spock
The Dark Crystal	Star Trek IV: The Voyage Home
E.T.	The Journey of Natty Gann
Escape to Witch Mountain	The Karate Kid
Indiana Jones and the	The Karate Kid (2)
Temple of Doom	The Karate Kid (3)
Jeremiah Johnson	The Last Starfighter
Lady and the Tramp	The Neverending Story
Mary Poppins	The Parent Trap
My Fair Lady	The Point
Oliver!	The Pride of the Yankees
Pippi Longstocking	The Red Balloon
Pollyanna	The Thief of Bagdad
Popeye	Who Framed Roger Rabbit?
Return of the Jedi	The Wind in the Willows
Rikki Tikki Tavi	The Wiz
Secret of NIMH	Yellow Submarine

Summer Safety

The best way to teach summer safety is by involving your child in a complete learning process. Practicing for specific situations will make your child better prepared when something really goes wrong. Talking with your child about summer safety will help her understand the dangers she may face and ways she can protect herself. Both talking and doing are essential for your safety program.

Talk frankly and often about safety, and listen patiently to your child's fears or concerns. What she is afraid of is just as important as what you are afraid of, and sometimes your kid just has to voice a fear to overcome it. When children tell you what they're sacred of—a ghost in the closet or a monster in the basement—take them seriously. Investigate the fears together—maybe even while holding hands—and deal with the "imaginary" dangers as well as the "real" ones.

The way you approach "real" fears is important. For instance, a major concern for all parents is strangers approaching their children. You could just tell your child to "stay away from strangers" in an authoritative voice, and give no further explanation. The tone will deliver the message, but it won't relieve fears or provide useful background information to a child under stress. In fact, it may just make your child more scared, since she won't know what she's supposed to be scared of.

Look closely at the statement: "Stay away from strangers!" There is no definition of what a stranger is. Children might assume that a stranger is anyone they haven't been introduced to. Try to see the advice you give from your child's perspective, and make sure you define words he might not understand. In this instance, suggest to your child that he ask himself these questions: "Do I know this person's name?" "Have I seen this person before?" and "Do I know what this person does in the community?" Try role-playing this situation to help children memorize these questions. If the answer to all these questions is "no," then the person really is a stranger.

Talking about summer dangers can help your family come up with guidelines and procedures for dealing with potential safety problems. Conversations about these dangers and guidelines will prepare your child to act appropriately when problems arise. A few potential dangers could be:

TALK ABOUT
AND PRACTICE
SUMMER SAFETY
AND MAKE
A SAFETY KIT

* Swimming accidents at the pool, lake, or beach.
* Fires from the stove, furnace, appliances, or matches.
* Accidents and injuries, such as serious cuts, burns, poisonings, falls, choking; a car, bike, or sports accidents.
* Boating accidents.
* Overexposure to the sun—burns or sun poisoning.
* Trouble with other people: children getting mugged or being followed home, break-ins, children witnessing someone breaking into a neighbor's house, strangers coming to the door, crank calls, or strangers asking if parents are home.
* Problems outside the house: losing keys, getting lost, or having a bike stolen.
* Fights with siblings or other neighborhood children.

Unfortunately, talking about dangers does not mean that children (or grownups) will know exactly how to respond to every emergency. But thinking about problems, giving your child solutions in advance, and *practicing* what to do when possible gives a child some emotional and cognitive poise when the inevitable crises do occur.

Some schools and community organizations offer safety programs that allow children to practice handling emergency situations. Some classes also teach basic first-aid skills, ways to arrange time spent alone, or methods of coping with potential dangers and fear. Investigate the options; children learn better in behavioral programs where they actively rehearse handling emergencies than in discussion groups where they stay seated. As you discuss with your child what he must learn about safety, you may need to help him adapt lessons to your own home, which may have different escape routes, for example. Go over safety procedures frequently. Even children who participate in safety programs forget their safety skills after a few months.

You should also consider making a kid's safety kit with your child this summer.

Description of a Child's Summer Safety Kit

This kit can be an important tool for your child. If she walks to the park or spends time alone at home, it can be particularly reassuring.

Use making the kit as an opportunity for learning. As you put the kit together, you and your child should discuss each component's function. Use a small box, such as a casette box, compact, or jewelry box. The kit should include:

+ Change for emergency phone calls
+ Money for transportation such as a cab
+ A medical identification card
+ A house key
+ A list of telephone numbers, including parents' work places, neighbors, relatives, and the police
+ A nutritious snack or even some candy
+ A small item to play with while waiting for parents to come home or a bus to arrive
+ A note: "I love you!"

☞ *Remember: Do not label the kit or key. Do not list your home telephone number. Keep all telephone numbers current. Refill and update the kit periodically.*

Children's safety is a family matter. Together you and your child can develop strategies for protecting her from harm, whether you're right beside her, in another room, or out of the house. Everyone will be more relaxed and confident about your child's independence if fears have been confronted and if everyone understands the family's rules and guidelines for safety.

Afterword: Was This Your Celebrated Summer Time?

Remember the school gym? The one everyone streamed out of on their way to the lockers at the beginning of this book? You're standing there alone now, watching the dirty-gray doors swing back and forth, back and forth after the last laughing kid.

Alone in the gym, your voice echoes off the walls and bounces back to you. The plastic fold-out chairs would make the place seem more comfortable if it weren't so huge. The ceiling seems very far away.

There's an implied threat to summer: "My child has to have the best time ever and be involved in meaningful activities for the next three months, or else." It's enough to make you feel alone and uncomfortable at times during the summer months. All parents at times, feel a little inadequate.

This book is not the be-all, end-all solution to that fear. I've felt and reflected on that fear myself. It *is* a series of steps that will put your child and the rest of your family in the gym with you—making decisions, dealing with setbacks, and enjoying the high points of summer together. The book gives you the frame of a summer; it's up to you and your family to fill in the rest of the picture, your way.

What counts is not that you read every word in the book (though if you're reading these, you've done a pretty good job), it's that you and your child are happy. What counts is *your* family deciding that this was a summer worth celebrating.

SAVE MEMENTOS LIKE POSTCARDS, SUMMER PHOTOS, AND TICKET STUBS TO REMEMBER YOUR SUMMER

Planning a successful summer is more like digging a tunnel than riding a bicycle. Rather than an easy ride from June to September with your child in the back seat it's a collaborative effort that will deepen your knowledge of your child and your child's knowledge of the world. It doesn't involve following colored lines on a map; rather, it's a trip that involves some guessing, some good luck, and a lot of love. And in the end, when you look back over the (w)hole you've made, what counts is your judgment—not that of the countless stopwatches and yardsticks by which our lives are measured.

Now is the time to stick to your convictions, to trust your intuitions, to get excited, to try to do something in a new way. Help your child take a leap and you leap too. Eventually enthusiasm pays off—it will succeed. Don't insist on waiting for the "perfect" solution and end up waiting out your child's middle years, because memories of these years and these summers become an indelible part of your child's adult personality and lifelong interests. The richness of childhood provides material for later life: strength of purpose, a sense of having alternatives, and vivid imagery.

It is my conviction that helping children use their time meaningfully is an investment in the future. Together you can make this time so rich that its effects reverberate throughout your child's life. You, as a parent, have many gifts to offer your child; I urge you to give freely and without expectations—your child will be grown and gone before you realize it. Take advantage of the time when they still need you, and not the other way around.

Good luck and have a wonderful summer. Write me and tell me about it.

Joan M. Bergstrom

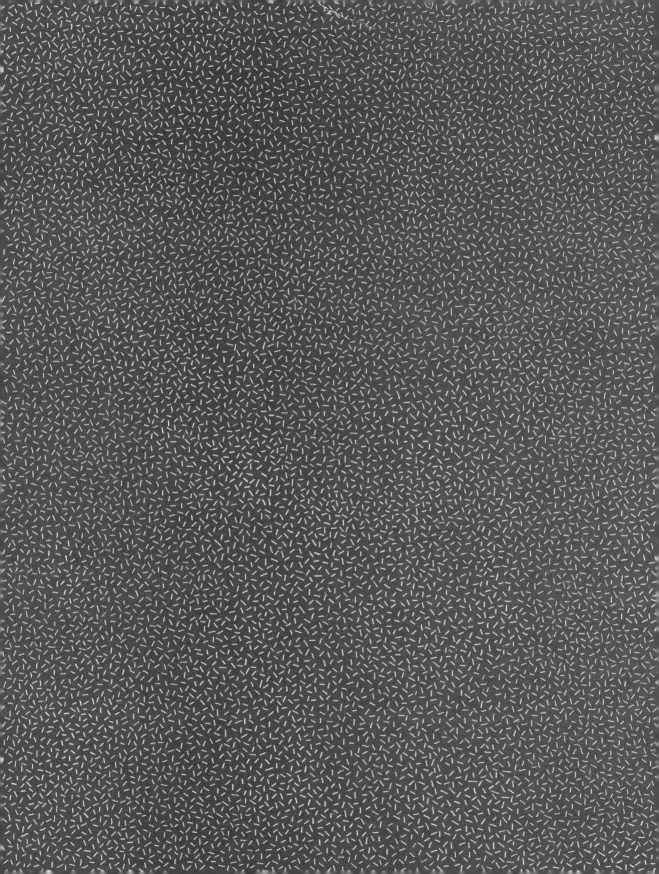

Appendix

Family Vacations

Super Family Vacations: Resort and Adventure Guide

> Martha Shirk and Nancy Klepper
> New York: Harper Collins, 1991

Great Vacations With Your Kids: The Complete Guide for Family Vacations in the U.S. for Infants to Teenagers

> Dorothy Ann Jordon and Marjorie Adoff Cohen
> New York: E.P. Dutton, 1990 (2nd edition)

Daytrips, Getaway Weekends and Vacations in the Mid-Atlantic States

> Patricia and Robert Foulke
> Chester, Connecticut: Grove Pequot Press, 1991 (2nd edition)

Directory of Free Vacation and Travel Information

> Raymond Carlson, editor
> New York: Pilot Books, annual

The Campground Directory

> Lake Bluff, Illinois: Woodall Publishing Co. (annual)
> (to order call (312) 295 7799)

Family Resorts of the Northeast: Carefree Vacations for All Ages, Including Mom and Dad

> Nancy Metcalf
> Woodstock, Vermont: The Countryman Press, 1991

Vacation!

> Nancy Hyden Woodward
> New York: Penguin Books, 1980

Camping in the National Park System and Lesser Known Areas of the National Park System.

> Superintendent of Documents,
> U.S. Government Printing Office,
> Washington, D.C. 20402

Families Welcome!

> Janet Tice
> Call (919) 489 2555 or (800) 326 0724
> 21 W. Colony Place, Durham, NC, 27705.

Summer Camps

A Smart Parents' Guide to Summer Camp

> Sheldon Silber
> New York: Farrar, Straus, Giroux, 1990

Summer Camps and Programs: Over 250 of the Best for Children 8 to 18

> Alice Goldsmith and Adrienne Lansing
> New York: Harmony, 1983

Guide to Accredited Camps

> American Camping Association
> Martinville, Indiana (annual)
> To order call (800) 426-CAMP

Summer Activities

Steven Caney's Invention Book

> Steven Caney
> New York: Workman Publishing Co., Inc., 1983

Steven Caney's Playbook

> Steven Caney
> New York: Workman Publishing Co., Inc., 1975

Steven Caney's Kids' America

>Steven Caney
>New York: Workman Publishing Co., Inc., 1978

Exploring Summer

>Sandra Market
>New York: Avon, 1987

All the Best Contests for Kids

>Joan M. Bergstrom and Craig Bergstrom
>Berkeley, California: Ten Speed Press, 1992 (3rd edition)

The Penny Whistle™ Party Planner

>Meredith Brokaw and Anne Gilbar
>New York: Weidenfield & Nicolson, 1987

Kid Camping from Aaaaiii! to Zip

>Patrick McManus
>New York: Avon, 1988

The Way Things Work

>David Macaulay
>Tucson, Arizona: Zephyr Press, 1988

What to Do With Kids on a Rainy Day

>Adrienne Katz
>New York: St. Martin's Press, 1987

As the Crow Flies: A First Book of Maps

>Gail Hartman
>New York: Bradbury Press, 1991

Creative Play Areas

Nonia Kosanke and Nena Warner

Nashville, Tennessee: School-Age NOTES, 1990

The Activities Club

Dear Parent,

"I'm bored. I'm bored. I'm bored." Every child, even the most active, has said it, and every parent has heard it, and wondered what to do.

What You As a Parent Can Do...

Helping your child discover his or her natural abilities, and then reinforcing those abilities is what we all strive to do as parents. But the main goal is to have FUN doing it!

The Activities Club helps your child to develop lifelong hobbies and to explore new interests. Club members receive activity kits in the mail, such as: Photography, Magic, The Universe, Birds, Mask Making, Cooking, Sea Life, Making Gifts, Games, and more. Each kit includes an exciting project, a club letter full of information, activity cards with games and contests, an iron-on badge, and lots of surprises.

The Activities Club was created to make your job easier and more rewarding. The Club provides fascinating projects and activities designed to appeal to your child's sense of curiosity, exploration, and most of all, fun!

For Kids Only...

The Activities Club is for boys and girls, ages 6 to 12. It is **their** club. Every aspect of The Club has been designed to recognize and reward their **involvement** and **initiative**. Each member has opportunities to enter contests, send away for free-bies, have their work published, contribute activity ideas, get mail back from The Club, and much, much more. It's truly interactive!

Of the kids, by the kids, and for the kids, The Activities Club helps children develop a sense of belonging, but also an equally important sense of self-direction and self-esteem!

Here's How It Works...

Sign up for The Activities Club now and your child will start to receive Activities Club Kits weekly or monthly in the mail. If you use the order form in the back of this book, you can save over $7.00 and get the book *All the Best Contests for Kids*(3rd edition) free. Choose a series of six or twelve kits, or try them individually. Kids love getting their own mail, so the fun begins the minute each package arrives.

Please take a moment to look at the enclosed brochure and description of kits. Then return the order form or call to order. Enroll your child in The Activities Club today. Let your child discover a whole new world of interests right in your home this summer.

Sincerely, Joan Bergstrom
President

P.S. FREE BONUS when you pay for a series of twelve kits we'll send you a FREE copy of *All the Best Contests For Kids*, and *winner of the 1990 Parents' Choice Award-Doing and Learning*.

P.P.S. Call 1-800-873-5487 now to enroll your child today!

The Activities Club is an innovative program that introduces school-age children to exciting hobbies. Every month, or weekly during the summer, club members receive kits in the mail acquainting them with fascinating new subjects, such as photography, magic, astronomy, and bird-watching. Each kit includes a terrific project, club letter, activity cards, iron-on badge, and more. Members also receive awards and birthday greetings. Through the club letter, members participate in contests and share ideas with members across the country.

Descriptions of Activity Kits:

The Welcome To The Club Kit contains an official club T-shirt, fabric markers, a poster, a top secret door hanger and an "official member" iron-on theme badge. Everything comes in a storage box which is perfect for keeping club stuff. The club letter has directions for children to set up their own clubs, while activity cards have tips on how to design secret club codes, make club snacks, and more.

The Photography Kit has a 35-mm camera, film, club letter, activity cards, iron-on camera badge, and a "Do Not Disturb" sign. The club letter is packed with information on picture-taking and experimenting with photography. Activity cards describe how to mount and frame a photo and create a family "picture" tree.

The Magic Kit has four magic tricks, magic wand, book of tricks, and an iron-on badge. The club letter focuses on the history of magic and the lives of famous magicians. Activity cards describe how to perform coin and card tricks and how to make props for magic shows.

The Safari Rubber Stamps Kit features a set of six wild animal stamps, inkpad, glitter glue, and giraffe iron-on badge. There is also a frame for master creations and several puzzles to create one's own. Activity cards explain how to make stationery and wrapping paper, create comic strips, and enter postcard contests.

The Bird Kit has a wooden bird feeder, bird chart, iron-on bird badge, and bird seed. The club letter has tips on bird-watching, while activity cards contain directions for making bird mobiles and bird baths. There are also directions for over 15 easy-to-make bird feeders.

The Mask Kit has materials to make African and cat masks, and also contains a mask iron-on badge. The club letter and activity cards offer directions for a variety of additional masks including papier mâché and theater masks.

The Universe Kit features a glow-in-the-dark map of the Universe and Glow Stars, as well as a star iron-on badge. The club letter has information about stars and constellations, and an interview with a space shuttle astronaut.

The Sea Life Kit features a wooden shark model, miniature squid, Undersea World Rummy cards, and sea life iron-on badge. The club letter is packed with information about sea life and The Cousteau Society, while activity cards contain additional projects, such as a sailor's valentine and sea mobile.

The Cooking Kit has an ice cream maker, chef's apron, materials to make chef's hats, measuring set and cooking tools, and an iron-on badge. The club letter has tips for planning and cooking healthy menus. Activity cards are full of great recipes for drinks, crunchy snacks, ice cream and frozen treats, salads, and fun meals.

The Gift Kit contains materials to make creative gifts for grandparents, parents, relatives, teachers, and friends. It includes Pour and Paint ® molds for decorative magnets, ornaments, pins and pendants, as well as fabric and patterns for making puppets. It also features a club letter, iron-on badge and activity cards full of additional gift-making projects.

The Games Kit features terrific games to play indoors and out, including Shut the Box, Bubble Fingers, marbles, and a tan-

gram. The club letter tells about the history of games, how to make a rainy day game box, and much more. Activity cards have games from around the world, and how to make up your own games.

The Nature's Treasures Kit has a fantastic new full color poster of an African rain forest. It also contains other exciting projects like making biodegradable soaps, all-natural toothpaste, and more. The club letter is packed with information on how children can help protect our world.

The key word in The Club is "active." Active members enjoy fun-filled indoor and outdoor activities with each kit. The Club stamps out boredom during afternoons, evenings, weekends, and vacations!

MEMBERSHIP FORM

CHILD'S NAME _____

BIRTHDAY _____

STREET _____

CITY/STATE/ZIP _____

PHONE NUMBER _____

☐ I have enclosed $13.95 plus $2.95 shipping and handling for The Welcome To The Club Kit. Shipments to MA add $.70 tax. I understand my child will receive kits on a regular basis unless I choose to cancel our membership.

☐ I have enclosed payment of $99.00 which includes shipping & handling for a series of 6 Activity Kits. Shipments to MA add $4.95 tax.

☐ I have enclosed payment of $195.00 which includes shipping & handling for a series of 12 Activity Kits. Shipments to MA add $9.75 tax.

Please send me kits ☐ weekly or ☐ monthly.

FREE BONUS (with orders of 12 kits). *All The Best Contests For Kids*, 3rd edition (Winner of a 1990 Parents' Choice Award), contains hundreds of fun and challenging contests on subjects from Music, Photography, and Math, to Rotten Sneakers! There is also a section on writing and getting published.

☐ Check Enclosed ☐ Mastercard ☐ VISA

CARD NUMBER _____

EXPIRATION DATE _____

ADULT'S NAME _____

STREET _____

CITY/STATE/ZIP _____

PHONE NUMBER _____

GIFT CARD MESSAGE _____

_____

THE ACTIVITIES CLUB ®
P.O. Box 9104
Waltham, MA 02254-9104

1-800-873-5487 CALL FOR FASTER SERVICE!